PRAISE FOR
LEAVING PLANET SIMPLE

Sustainability executives are bombarded with a flood of advice, much of which is preaching to the choir. *Leaving Planet Simple* is different. Authored by a highly educated resilience scientist with real-world business experience, it is a thought-provoking book that offers profound insight into revamping business paradigms to navigate the uncertainty and variability of a changing planet. A key insight is the importance of integrating sustainability into foundational corporate strategy, decision-making, and value creation to build corporate resilience. Dr. Gold does a remarkable job to distill complex concepts into actionable advice that resonates with experienced executives. The book is a must-read for business leaders seeking to transform their organizations to succeed in the twenty-first century.

—Diane Kappas
Retired VP, Global Sustainability
Fortune 200 materials company

Leaving Planet Simple stands out in the increasingly crowded field of corporate sustainability literature. The book offers a rare combination of practical business tips and deep research into the why of today's sustainability movement. It's a must-read guide penned by a legitimate expert. Highly recommended for directors and executives who want to transform sustainability from charity into competitive advantage.

—Simon Shakesheff
Non Executive Director

Leaving Planet Simple is an essential guide for business leaders trying to make sense of what corporate sustainability means. I especially like how Dr. Gold sets out the various Planet Simple traps that affect businesses today and what they can do about it. In my decades of experience in corporate strategy and governance, I've come to know that sustainability is about transforming mindsets—and this book explains exactly how to do it.

—Gib Hedstrom
Founder, ESG Navigator

Mankind's hubris in assuming dominion over nature has been disproven countless times, from Gilgamesh to the Dust Bowl. Yet, even today, people are burning the planet's lungs to produce palm oil and beef. Who is accountable? Who should be? How can change occur? (It must!)

Corporations control the majority of the global economy. As the beneficiaries of the natural environment, it falls to them to lead a paradigm shift.

Dr. Gold candidly explains the folly of the simplistic approach, cutting through the clutter of "ESG" and other nomenclature. He lays out an enlightened approach beneficial to business and the planet alike.

Dr. Gold applies resilience science to both the natural and corporate environments. Even the term "re-silience" is inherently reactive; it involves preparation to rebound from an adverse occurrence. Let's hope readers and the corporate world embrace the necessity of "pre-silience."

—Douglas Hileman, FSA, CRMA, CPEA, PE
Coauthor, COSO's "Achieving Effective Internal Control over Sustainability Reporting (ICSR)"

President, Douglas Hileman Consulting LLC

A timely work that expertly blends scientific theory with grounded practice, *Leaving Planet Simple* provides much needed guidance for those seeking sustainable corporate futures. The volume provides ways for businesses to rapidly course-correct while navigating sustainability in an increasingly volatile world. Dr. Gold's advice is based on established research into complex dynamic systems, a deeply necessary approach for business as it grapples with systemic challenges from the local to the global. The book is an indispensable resource for business leaders seeking to learn their way through the complex challenges of the twenty-first century.

—Professor Lance Gunderson
Editor, Applied Panarchy
Professor, Emory University

Leaving Planet Simple is a book we all need now. Dr. Gold explains why we are stuck in ways of thinking that no longer serve us and how to move forward in simple, practical ways. Why? Because we are in a state of deep dissonance today. We are already experiencing the effects of climate change. Our news feeds give us constant input on the polycrisis of climate change, human conflict, and human burnout. Yet we resist leading the fundamental change necessary. As Dr. Gold says, the blueprint for this change is leaving Planet Simple so we can learn to thrive on Planet Earth.

—Karimah Hudda
Founder and Chief Catalyst, illumine.earth

LEAVING
PLANET
SIMPLE

LEAVING
PLANET
SIMPLE

EMBRACING
SUSTAINABILITY,
ESG, AND **RESILIENCE** TO
TRANSFORM YOUR BUSINESS

DR. ALEX GOLD

Forbes | Books

Published by Forbes Books, Charleston, South Carolina.
An imprint of Advantage Media Group.

Forbes Books is a registered trademark, and the Forbes Books colophon is a trademark of Forbes Media, LLC.

Printed in the United States of America.

10 9 8 7 6 5 4 3 2 1

ISBN: 978-1-64225-699-4 (Hardcover)
ISBN: 978-1-64225-698-7 (eBook)

Library of Congress Control Number: 2024910226

Cover design by Analisa Smith.
Layout design by Ruthie Wood.

This custom publication is intended to provide accurate information and the opinions of the author in regard to the subject matter covered. It is sold with the understanding that the publisher, Forbes Books, is not engaged in rendering legal, financial, or professional services of any kind. If legal advice or other expert assistance is required, the reader is advised to seek the services of a competent professional.

Since 1917, Forbes has remained steadfast in its mission to serve as the defining voice of entrepreneurial capitalism. Forbes Books, launched in 2016 through a partnership with Advantage Media, furthers that aim by helping business and thought leaders bring their stories, passion, and knowledge to the forefront in custom books. Opinions expressed by Forbes Books authors are their own. To be considered for publication, please visit **books.Forbes.com**.

To my mother,

Susan Carol Elgin

To the memory of my father,

Stewart Benson Gold

To a bright future for

Sasha Gwen Ninkov

James Stevan Ninkov

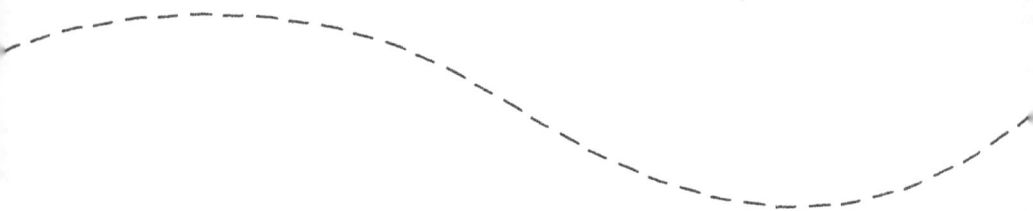

ACKNOWLEDGMENTS

In *Parable of the Sower*, Octavia Butler writes, "All that you change, changes you." This book is over a decade in the making, and it would take up all the space in this book to acknowledge everyone who has helped me to get to this point. It would make for a boring book—and so I would like to focus on those who have changed me by giving me the confidence to put the rest of these pages in print.

To Professor Michael Hood of Amherst College, who allowed me a rare opportunity to work as a true biologist so early in my career. To Michael, I owe my confidence as a scientist.

To Professor John Merson of the University of New South Wales, who introduced me to resilience science and opened my eyes to the importance of culture and paradigm on everything we do. To John, I owe my confidence as a philosopher and pragmatist.

To my professional colleagues through my corporate career, who were generous with their expertise and who gave me the opportunity to step up. To them, I owe my confidence as a business leader.

To the BWD North America team, who are so smart and dedicated to work anywhere but have chosen to work with me—I get a bit emotional any time I really stop to think about it. To the team, I owe my confidence as a mentor.

To Derryn, Luke, and Amy, who offered me an unmatched opportunity to take their brand to North America—the most rewarding challenge of my career. Thank you for seeing potential in me that I have not always seen in myself. To the Heilbuths, I owe my confidence as someone who has something to offer the world.

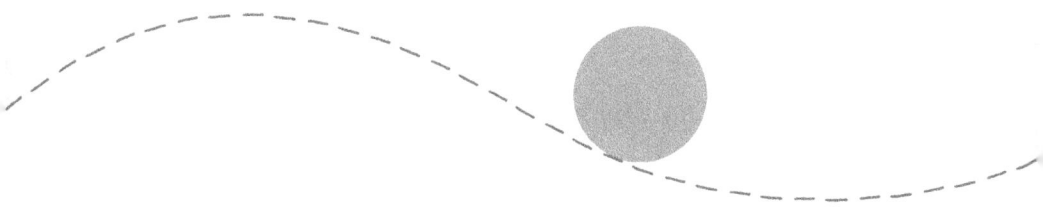

CONTENTS

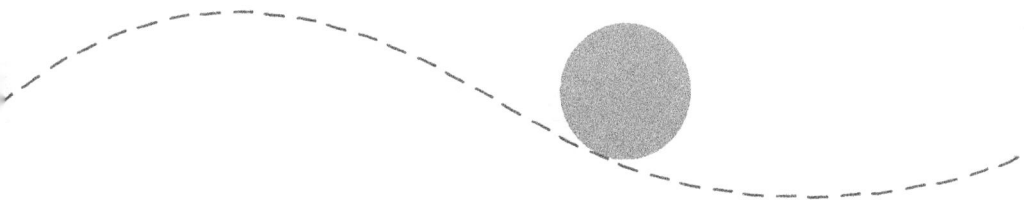

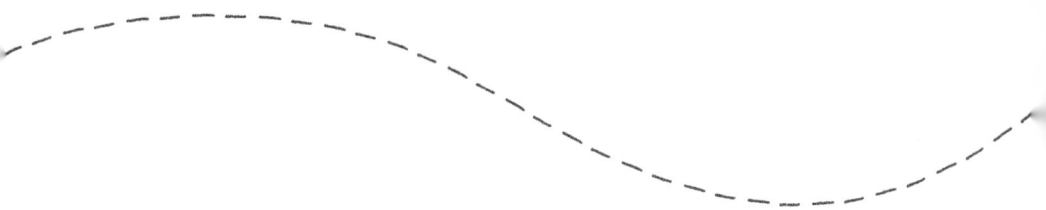

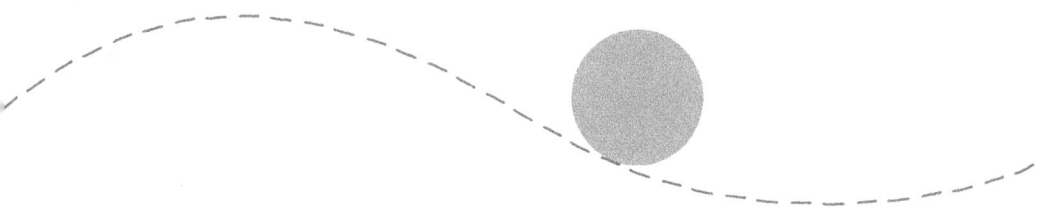

INTRODUCTION

> *Make everything as simple as possible,*
> *but no simpler.*
> —Albert Einstein

Since the dawn of humanity, we have approached life as individuals existing in our own worlds—isolated from other living creatures and indifferent to how our existence is interconnected to everything around us. By neglecting to factor in our relationships with other human beings, animals, ecosystems, and the planet at large, mounting global challenges indicate that something isn't quite right. Perhaps our worldview—our view of how the world works—is a bit too simple.

The late Stephen Hawking said that the solution to issues such as resource depletion, overpopulation, deforestation, and climate change is for humans to leave Planet Earth.[1] Hawking is not alone. Carl Sagan,[2] Jeff Bezos,[3] and many others have made similar suggestions.

In this book, I will make the argument that the solution is not to leave Planet Earth. Instead, we must leave what I call Planet Simple, a mechanical, reductionist, human-centered worldview that has dominated Western society since the Enlightenment. Leaving Planet

Simple does not involve rocket ships, but perhaps something more challenging—a paradigm shift in how we see ourselves, the world around us, and the organizations we lead.

The Planet Simple metaphor is inspired by Thomas Kuhn's *The Structure of Scientific Revolutions*.[4] Kuhn argues that scientific understanding does not progress in a linear, incremental fashion, as is commonly believed. Instead, scientific research occurs on a foundation of a commonly accepted paradigm, or mindset, of how the world works. Science goes deeper because its practitioners can take this foundational paradigm for granted—research depth would be impossible if researchers kept arguing over the basics. At some point, however, researchers encounter real-world anomalies that throw the field into crisis. Eventually, the awareness of anomaly lasts so long and penetrates so deeply that the only resolution is the adoption of a new paradigm. Kuhn himself is considered to have brought "paradigm shift"[5] into common use.

Paradigm shifts are never just increments to what is already known. They require the reconstruction of prior theory and reevaluation of prior fact—an intrinsically revolutionary process. When the transition is complete, the profession will have changed its view of the field, its methods, and its goals. Kuhn goes so far as to claim that after a paradigm shift, it is as if we had been suddenly transported to another planet. Referring to the Copernican revolution, he states, "The very ease and rapidity with which astronomers saw new things when looking at old objects with old instruments may make us wish to say that, after Copernicus, astronomers lived in a different world."[6]

We think we live in a different world—Planet Simple—and this mistake is the root cause of the issues noted by Hawking. Leaving Planet Simple, however, requires a paradigm shift that is already facing resistance from established stakeholders comfortable with the prevailing paradigm. According to Kuhn, this resistance is typical of paradigm shifts. To apply his words to our own subject matter, Kuhn may suggest that these stakeholders will convince themselves that they can fit the reality of Planet Earth "into the inflexible box supplied by [Planet Simple]."[7]

Paradigm shifts never occur overnight, nor as the result of one person. Rather, they occur when enough of us consider that something is amiss and are thus prepared to see the world differently.

And something is indeed amiss. An existing paradigm falls into crisis when its current explanations deteriorate and the universal agreement over fundamentals is called into question. In recent decades, many varied propositions have been put into place as to the "purpose" of business or how its success should be measured. According to Kuhn, arguments over basic premises such as purpose and success are symptomatic of a field in crisis.[8]

To address a crisis of this magnitude, this book offers a new way of looking at all the elements in play. It can be read by anyone interested in business strategy, regardless of whether they consider themselves to be a sustainability practitioner. The message will be understood best, though, by those who are curious. Perhaps you're not much of a sustainability "believer" or otherwise consider yourself "core business," but you've picked up this book because you're curious about why the sustainability trend has remained so persistent. Perhaps you're later in your career and interested in how you can see sustainability as an opportunity to leave a positive legacy.

Or perhaps you come to this book already well-versed in sustainability but curious about how to break through persistent blockages plaguing corporate sustainability efforts. Curious about how to spot the traps that sustainability efforts fall into, when they are (often unintentionally) twisted to just be more of the same, rather than the transformation that they need to be. I'll introduce you to many of these Planet Simple traps throughout this book—and explain how to avoid them.

A key hurdle for corporate sustainability is that most do not recognize the *necessity* of change. Sustainability is seen as an extra; not necessary for the day-to-day and a (perceived) financial burden. This book seeks to turn this argument on its head. By suggesting that businesses today are stuck on Planet Simple, I am saying that businesses are, by default, in need of a course correction to get to Planet Earth. Corporate sustainability is the discipline underpinning the course correction. It is not an option that businesses can take if they are feeling charitable or enjoy "doing good"—it is the *only* option for ongoing success into the future.

There are many views on what is meant by sustainability, environment, social, and governance (ESG), and resilience, and I will not offer my own definitions here. I don't see them as independent matters. Instead, I see them as different names given to the underlying paradigm shift underway in business today. Trying to distinguish between them is like the parable of the blind people touching different parts of the elephant and concluding that they are feeling a nose, or a trunk, or a tail, when they are all in fact touching the elephant. Whether we call it sustainability, ESG, or resilience, success relies on leaving Planet Simple and rewiring business for the reality of Planet Earth.

Although this is my view (and I hope yours by the time you finish the book), I will attempt to be clear and consistent throughout the text. Rather than using terms interchangeably, I will tend toward:

- using "corporate sustainability" to refer to the emerging practice of integrating ESG considerations into company strategy and operations

- using "ESG investing" to refer to a specific type of investing practice (reserved mostly to chapter 3)

- using "resilience science" to refer to empirical research that offers the scientific foundation for a worldview better suited to reality than Planet Simple

I've organized the book into three parts. Part I introduces Planet Simple. If you are going to move your organization from the mindset of Planet Simple, it's crucial to understand where it came from and how it is so embedded in modern business management. The name Planet Simple comes from an initialism that helps us remember some of its S-I-M-P-L-E assumptions:

S TABLE
the world is *stable* over time

I NDIVIDUAL
people are *individuals* by nature and the world can be understood by breaking it up into individual pieces for analysis

M EASURABLE
we can *measure* system components

P REDICTABLE
we can *predict* future system states

L INEAR
change proceeds in a *linear* fashion

E QUILIBRIUM
forces tend to balance each other to achieve an *equilibrium*

Starting at biblical times, we will venture through the Enlightenment and up to today, all the while understanding how Planet Simple has come to dominate how we live. We will uncover how the Planet Simple mindset goes hand-in-hand with business objectives of control and efficiency. We will explore how Planet Simple has been challenged of late and introduce today's calls for businesses to pivot from efficiency to resilience. We will also unpack how ESG investing as a solution to today's global challenges was flawed from the start yet remains a sign of the fundamental paradigm shift underway from Planet Simple to Planet Earth.

Part II is the intellectual fulcrum of the book, diving deep into the paradigm change needed to transform business management for the real world. There is a crash course on resilience science, the research that introduced us to tipping points and disproved every S-I-M-P-L-E assumption underpinning Planet Simple. We will go over the revolutionary concept of panarchy—a theory backed by empirical observation of change in complex systems—that helps us understand how humans have *scaled up* to catalyze global change. This section explains the ultimate trap of Planet Simple: how we can be lured into a false sense of stability because we fail to consider changes over wider scales of space and time.

It also explains how decision-making on Planet Simple results in bad business outcomes through fake certainty (or *spurious certitude*, as resilience scientists would put it) and a failure to learn, and it offers the intellectual underpinning for how to take advantage of uncertainty and create a learning organization—setting up the practical guidance in Part III.

Part III offers the practical tools for managing for the reality of Planet Earth. It offers a framework for understanding how sustainability has always been part of your value creation strategy. It describes tools for integrating sustainability into strategy and governance, including scenario analysis guidance. Finally, it explains how you can turn the *burden* of reporting into a strategic imperative, and why transforming the reporting process is fundamental for meeting emerging requirements to manage for *resilience*.

Before getting into it, I'll offer a view as to how my experience led me to write the pages that follow. My original passion was biology, specifically genetics and cellular behavior from individual levels to complex ecosystems. After some time sequencing DNA, peering into microscopes, and publishing scientific papers, I had a desire—like many other scientists—to explore how things are done outside the lab.

I was fortunate to receive an Australian Government scholarship to complete a PhD as an international student at the University of New South Wales. Admittedly, I recall accepting the offer more for the opportunity to live and study in Australia than thinking it would shape my entire future. This PhD track was one that is increasingly rare today: an opportunity to dive deep into the philosophy of how knowledge is generated and used (as opposed to being an underpaid research assistant on a predetermined project). The philosophy I'm speaking of is not abstract navel gazing—far from it. I was embedded in a government agency tasked to integrate climate change into its strategic planning and, keenly acquainted with how resilience science had disproved S-I-M-P-L-E assumptions, I was confident of success.

But I, like the resilience scientists before me, uncovered barriers preventing the agency from adjusting its practices to the reality of climate change. The barriers were not a lack of knowledge or interest within the agency. As I will explain in this book, it was Planet Simple at play—and its reach presents barriers to any organization seeking to transform to meet today's global challenges.

Although resilience science better describes reality, it is a relatively recent development compared with the Planet Simple mindset that has guided our species for millennia. In the years since my government agency experience, I have worked in the corporate sector as companies face increasing pressure to integrate environmental and social change into their strategies. Over these years, I was able to gain practical experience not just identifying Planet Simple traps but also overcoming them. The most successful companies weren't those with the most money, but those who recognized the paradigm shift needed to get to Planet Earth.

This book aims to offer both the practical guidance of *what* is needed and the academic depth of *why* it is needed. My motivation is to help business leaders who may recognize that something is broken but haven't (yet) been able to articulate it. Sustainability professionals face a similar challenge, thrust into consistent arguments that their work is not "core business"—an assumption rooted in a failure to recognize the deficiencies of today's Planet Simple mindset and the *necessity* of change.

These leaders are the Copernicus of our age.

Like Copernicus, these changemakers face an avalanche of resistance. My efforts here aim to support change by calling out the ubiquity of Planet Simple thinking and suggesting practical tools to get businesses to Planet Earth. There are certain insights that, once you see them, begin to seep into your experience of daily living. The Planet Simple mindset is one of them. Once you know how it works and how it contrasts with the reality of Planet Earth, you will see how it explains current decision-making of individuals, businesses, and government—and why Planet Simple thinking is to blame for the myriad challenges presently facing the world. This awareness is the precondition for change.

Let's get started.

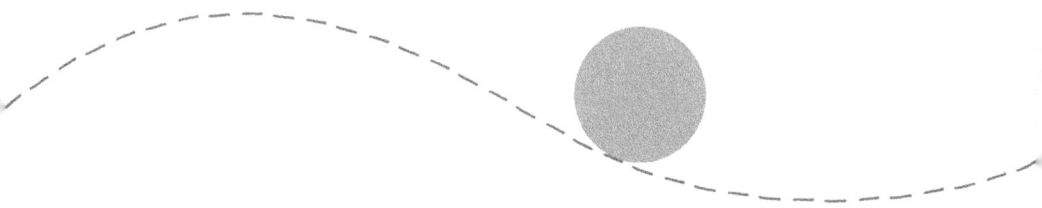

PART I:

Planet Simple

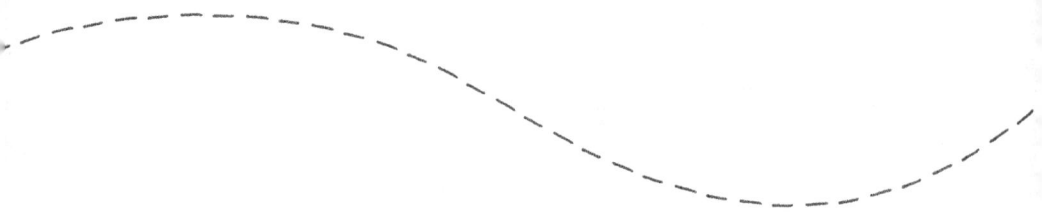

CHAPTER 1

Planet Simple's Dominance

> *Let us make mankind in our image, in our likeness,*
> *so that they may rule over the fish in the sea and the*
> *birds in the sky, over the livestock and all the wild*
> *animals, and over all the creatures that move along*
> *the ground.*
>
> —Genesis 1:26

Welcome to Planet Simple

Until the "truth" of Earth's place in the cosmos was thrown into crisis, our understanding looked markedly different. Egyptian astronomer Claudius Ptolemy set the stage in the second century CE, with his geocentric model of the universe that held Earth as the stationary center, orbited by the sun and other planets. This all seemed reasonable and as the Ptolemaic system was generally accurate in celestial predictions, it was accepted for centuries without question.

Things changed, however, as astronomic observations became more precise and scholars noticed discrepancies in the Ptolemaic model, inspiring new but not widely accepted ideas of a heliocentric model (sun-centered). Along came Nicolaus Copernicus in the early sixteenth century, who turned the Ptolemaic model on its head, standing behind his research and view of the sun as the center of the solar system, with Earth and other planets orbiting around it. Copernicus's work questioned man's place in the universe with an explanation that better accounted for reality, and inspired a seismic paradigm shift in scientific thought that laid the foundation for Galileo's observations, Newtonian physics, and the Scientific Revolution as a whole.

The Planet Simple mindset, long taken as the "truth," has shaped what we assume and believe is the way things are. But a world attempting to function in near constant crises demands we question "the way things are" to recognize our authentic place versus assumptions.

A Brief Chronicle of Planet Simple

Planet Simple has a long history with its roots in the Scientific Revolution of the sixteenth and seventeenth centuries. At its core was a belief, derived from the Bible, that human beings had dominion over nature, that indeed the natural world was created by God for the benefit of humankind. Led by leading thinkers such as Francis Bacon, creator of the scientific method, or René Descartes, the founder of "rationalism," science and technology were considered human innovations that could be used to harness the fruits of nature to serve the needs of humans. They further believed that there were certain "laws of nature" that could be understood and mastered.

The Scientific Revolution led to the Enlightenment of the seventeenth and eighteenth centuries and the creation of the modern, liberal, democratic state. Human beings were no longer "God's children" or vassals of a king, but independent, autonomous, and rational actors with certain "inalienable rights." It was a radical departure from how society had been organized for more than a millennium and drew its inspiration from the democratic ideals of ancient Greece and Rome. Political autonomy was followed by economic autonomy as individuals, acting in their own best interest, would lead to the optimal allocation of goods, labor, and capital.

The Enlightenment led to the Industrial Revolution of the eighteenth and nineteenth centuries with its radical advancements in technology to increase the production of "useful" goods derived from natural resources. Eventually, in the twentieth century, ideas that had been used to increase the productivity of machines were applied directly to the productivity of humans.

These ideas had a profound impact on the world. The Scientific Revolution, the Enlightenment, the Industrial Revolution all led to advancements in human well-being, a greater understanding of the natural world and human health, increases in life expectancy and personal wealth, more time for leisure activities, and, most importantly, the first recognition that citizens—if not all of them—had certain rights. But all these developments took place atop a flawed foundation—Planet Simple—the flaws of which are increasingly apparent.

Given that history, what is *mindset* and why is it so important? Our mindset is the shared rules, assumptions, and points of view that we hold about how the world works. Because of the complexity of our world, our mindset has to be a generalized picture of how everything fits together. Mindset is so important because everything we do is underpinned by its assumptions or generalizations. These assumptions aren't inherently bad. They help us make sense of a much more complex reality. The world is complex and unpredictable. Naturally (or rather unnaturally), we try to simplify it and predict it.

It's important to understand mindset if you want to change it. Simply stated, people won't change their minds unless they feel like they need to change, and they won't feel like they need to change unless they realize their current approach is incorrect in some way. Let's now dig deeper into the Planet Simple mindset that has come to dominate our world today—and why it needs to change.

	PLANET SIMPLE
How We Think the World Works	Stability Individual Measurable Predictable Linear Equilibrium
How We Make Decisions	The world is fully knowable Certainty is possible
Business Objectives	Technical rationality Optimization Efficiency

ON PLANET SIMPLE, HUMANS CAN CONTROL NATURE

In Genesis 1:26, God said, "Let us make mankind in our image, in our likeness, so that they may rule over the fish in the sea and the birds in the sky, over the livestock and all the wild animals, and over all the creatures that move along the ground."[9]

The assumption, literally from on high, was that humans can and should control nature. It also implies that nature is stable enough to be controlled, and that "human" and "natural" systems are separate things.

These assumptions have dominated Western attitudes for over two millennia and are foundational to today's liberal democracies and capitalist economies. John Locke, one of the most influential Enlightenment thinkers and considered the father of liberalism, echoed this sentiment in stating that, "The Earth, and all that is therein, is given to Men for the Support and Comfort of their being."[10] In claiming mankind's dominion over the natural world, Locke referenced both "natural law" and the Bible and these ideas still guide Western attitudes.

Enlightenment thinker Francis Bacon was a key contributor to the scientific method. Bacon felt that by understanding nature, and using scientific instruments, man could govern or direct the natural work of nature to produce definitive results for mankind. His "ideal society" is one that has managed to bring nature to subjection via breakthroughs in science and technology.[11] By seeking knowledge of nature, man could have power over it.

It's hard to underestimate how the development of the scientific method changed the world and is still with us today. "It looms so large as the real origin, both of the modern world and of the modern mentality," wrote mid-twentieth-century historian Herbert Butterfield, of Bacon's scientific method. "It outshines everything since the rise of Christianity and reduces the Renaissance and the Reformation to the rank of mere episodes."[12]

ON PLANET SIMPLE HUMANS CAN KNOW THE "LAWS OF NATURE"

This assumption finds its source in the work of René Descartes, who followed from Bacon. Descartes was the first thinker to emphasize the use of reason to develop the natural sciences and his work led to the Age of Reason. He was also the impetus for the so-called "anthropocentric" revolution, in other words, the human being is set free, no longer just a child of God.[13] In modernity, the guarantor of truth is not God anymore, but human beings. This provided the basis for the Enlightenment thinkers like Rousseau and Voltaire who were to follow. Natural law led to natural rights, and this became the basis for the modern democratic state we know today.

The ideas of Bacon and Descartes still have a profound impact on our modern mindset. As Francis Fukuyama wrote in his recent book, *Liberalism and Its Discontents*:

> From its earliest beginnings, modern liberalism was strongly associated with a distinctive cognitive mode, that of modern natural science. This mode assumes that there is an objective reality outside the human mind, which human beings can gradually understand and ultimately come to manipulate. The fountainhead of this approach was the philosopher Rene Descartes, who began with the most radical skepticism about the existence of that external reality, and progressively worked his way towards a structured system by which it could be apprehended. That apprehension would come to be based on empirical observation and an experi-

mental method, pioneered by Francis Bacon, that sought to establish causality by controlling the observation of correlated events. This is the method upon which modern natural science is based, and is taught in every basic statistics course in the world today. Liberalism was thus strongly associated with the project of mastering nature through science and technology, and using the latter to bend the given world to suit human purposes.[14]

Leading thinkers advocated that these "laws of nature" could be understood by using reductionist methods. In other words, reduce natural systems to their component parts—and then the function of the system could be understood, not as a whole but by understanding its component parts. The concept of "emergent properties"—system characteristics or functions that emerge from the interaction of its components—was absent. The reality of emergent properties is the basis for the saying, "the whole is greater than the sum of its parts." To reductionists, the whole is equal to the sum of the parts. This is quite useful when designing and building a steam engine but falls apart completely when trying to manage a complex, dynamic system like a rainforest, a school, or a company. And yet we still try.

ON PLANET SIMPLE, HUMANITY ORIGINATED AS ISOLATED INDIVIDUALS

Three Enlightenment-era thought leaders—Thomas Hobbes, John Locke, and Jean-Jacques Rousseau—heavily influenced foundational ideas of Western society and, ultimately, its very identity with emphasis on knowledge, reason, and individual rights.

Hobbes explored the social contract concept in his seminal work, *Leviathan*, arguing that individuals would willingly give up some of their natural rights in exchange for security and order, which laid the groundwork for a strong central government and societal order.[15]

Locke's work became strong inspiration for America's founding fathers, focusing on natural rights such as life, liberty, and property and that if a central government failed to uphold its end of the social contract, citizens had the right to rebel. This concept went on to play a fundamental role in shaping the Declaration of Independence and the US Constitution.[16]

Shortly after Locke's time, Rousseau believed that individuals were inherently good but corrupted by society, which inspired his proposal of a direct democracy of individuals making collective decisions based on general will.[17]

Renowned political scientist Francis Fukuyama, however, relied on our core biology to disprove the Enlightenment assumption that we are all individuals by nature. From his epic *Political Order and Political Decay*:

> [Rousseau], Hobbes, and Locke were wrong on one very important point. All three thinkers say human beings in the state of nature as isolated individuals, for whom society was not natural. ... We might label this the Hobbesian fallacy: the idea that human beings were primordially individualistic and that they entered into society at a later stage in their development only as a result of a rational calculation that social cooperation was the best way for them to achieve their individual ends. This premise of primordial individualism underpins the understanding of rights contained in the American Declaration of Independence and thus of the democratic political community that springs from it. This premise also underlies contemporary neoclassical economics, which builds its models on the assumption that human

beings are rational beings who want to maximize their individual utility or incomes. … Everything that modern biology and anthropology tell us about the state of nature suggests the opposite: there was never a period in human evolution when human beings existed as isolated individuals.[18]

And yet the "isolated individual" forms the basis for classical economics, which still heavily influences both government policy and business management around the world today. In his highly influential work from 1776, *Wealth of Nations*, Adam Smith introduced the idea that individuals, acting in their own self-interest, could serve the greater good. The "invisible hand" was a metaphor for how individual decisions and actions in the market would lead to an optimal distribution of goods and services across society.[19] In more modern times, Milton Friedman, the free-market economist, developed what's known as the "Friedman Doctrine," based on his influential 1970 article in the New York Times: "The Friedman Doctrine: The Social Responsibility of Business Is to Increase Its Profits."[20]

According to the Friedman Doctrine, the political principle that underlies the market mechanism is unanimity. In an ideal free market resting on private property, no individual can coerce any other, all cooperation is voluntary, all parties to such cooperation benefit or they need not participate. There are no "social" values, no "social" responsibilities in any sense other than the shared values and responsibilities of individuals. Society is a collection of individuals and of the various groups they voluntarily form. Margaret Thatcher echoed this sentiment in 1987 when she famously said, "There's no such thing as society. There are just individual men and women, and there are families."[21]

PLANET SIMPLE IS AT EQUILIBRIUM

The invisible hand,[22] coined by Adam Smith, as we discussed above, is a metaphor for the unseen forces that move the free-market economy. Through individual self-interest and freedom of production and consumption, the best interests of society as a whole are fulfilled. This aligns with the reductionist worldview that things can be broken down into constituent parts and analyzed, and then pieced back together to create an understanding of the whole.

Many of these classical economic models assume a world of balancing forces that maintain equilibrium. Equilibrium goes hand-in-hand with stability. When we speak of assumptions of stability here, we're not saying that people assumed everything to stay the same all the time. But rather people assumed that any change that did occur was linear in nature and ultimately "balanced" such that the world tended to gravitate toward a single, predictable equilibrium state. We will pick this up again in detail in chapter 4, when comparing the Nature Balanced worldview with more realistic worldviews offered by resilience science.

These assumptions underpin the competitive equilibrium at the foundation of microeconomics. External shocks to supply and demand might disturb this equilibrium, but the price mechanism will ultimately stabilize it. In essence, price is a measure of scarcity; when a resource becomes scarce, the price increases. Consumers respond to this price increase by buying less, and producers respond by producing more or by developing substitutes.

This branch of traditional microeconomics focuses on prices serving as a negative feedback loop meant to maintain economic equilibrium in an ever-growing economy. In general, this ideology rejects any government interventions in markets, any limits to economic growth, or any possibility of the market economy transitioning to an alternative equilibrium state.[23]

By assuming the economy and other complex systems naturally gravitate to an equilibrium state, Planet Simple gives us comfort that there will always be some "natural" feedback loop that will "correct" any excesses and keep us on the right track. On Planet Simple, we don't need to worry about tipping points or irreversible consequences. In Part II, we will explore how these assumptions simply don't line up with our modern understanding of Planet Earth.

PLANET SIMPLE IS PREDICTABLE

Former options trader Nassim Nicholas Taleb became fascinated with this concept of looking at the past with presumably 20/20 vision. When catastrophic "outlier" events occurred in history, we often came up with simple explanations for them, ones that may have been comforting at the time but provided little insight that could lead to a greater ability to predict disaster in the future.

From 2001 to 2018, he published a series of five books on this topic, his most famous and influential being the 2007 *The Black Swan: The Impact of the Highly Improbable*.[24] Incredibly, the book was published just before the onset of the global financial crisis, an "outlier" event that very few predicted.[25] Of course, the book and later movie, *The Big Short*, provides an amazing example of the very few—but often ignored and ostracized—brave souls who did predict the coming collapse. Copernicus was also ignored and ostracized.

Taleb introduced the notion of a "narrative fallacy" to describe how flawed stories of the past shape our views of the world and our expectations for the future.[26] Narrative fallacies arise inevitably from our continuous attempt to make sense of the world. These explanatory stories that people find so compelling are simple; they are concrete rather than abstract; they assign a larger role to talent, stupidity, and intentions than to luck; and they focus on the random events that happened rather than on the countless events that failed to happen.

As Taleb pointed out in *The Black Swan*, our tendency to construct and believe coherent narratives of the past makes it difficult for us to accept the limits of our forecasting ability.[27] Everything makes sense in hindsight, a fact that financial pundits exploit every evening as they offer convincing accounts of the day's events. And we cannot suppress the powerful intuition that what makes sense in hindsight today was predictable yesterday. The illusion that we understand the past, combined with Planet Simple assumptions that the world is knowable, stable, and at equilibrium, fosters overconfidence in our ability to predict the future.

And yet, managing on Planet Simple, we persist with these assumptions, these illusions.

BUSINESS ON PLANET SIMPLE—THE COMFORT OF CERTAINTY

Traditional economic theory assumes perfect information and discounts or ignores what we don't know, a phenomenon that the father of behavioral economics, Daniel Kahneman, described as WYSIATI—What You See Is All There Is.[28]

WYSIATI combines with the narrative fallacy to generate an overconfidence that the future will be the same as the recent past. For example, Irving Fisher, a famous economist from the 1920s, just days before the market crash of 1929, stated that "stock prices have reached what looks like a permanently high plateau. I do not feel there will be soon, if ever, a 50- or 60-point break from present levels, such as (bears) have predicted. I expect to see the stock market a good deal higher within a few months."[29] The same pattern was to repeat itself in the run up to the 2008 financial crisis.

In his classic book, *Thinking, Fast and Slow*, Kahneman discusses the very human tendency to jump to conclusions based on very limited evidence, stating: "WYSIATI facilitates the achievement of coherence and of the cognitive ease that causes us to accept a statement as true. It explains why we can think fast, and how we are able to make sense of partial information in a complex world. Much of the time, the coherent story we put together is close enough to reality to support reasonable action. We often fail to allow for the possibility that evidence that should be critical to our judgement is missing—what we see is all there is (WYSIATI)."[30]

Kahneman points out that sustaining doubt is actually much harder work than falling into an easy, false sense of certainty. "It is easier to construct a coherent story when you know little, when there are fewer pieces to fit into the puzzle," he writes. "Our comforting conviction that the world makes sense rests on a secure foundation: our almost unlimited ability to ignore our ignorance."[31]

The core of this illusion, maintains Kahneman, is that we believe we understand the past. After all, hindsight is 20/20. This implies that the future should also be knowable, predictable, but in fact we understand the past far less than we think we do. We think we're looking backward with 20/20 vision, but instead it depends entirely on the glasses we are wearing.

We will talk further below about being more comfortable with the unknown, with the unpredictable, with not just a lack of data but of appreciating phenomena for which there is no data to be measured. This is all part of managing on Planet Earth rather than living with the comforting but spurious certitude of Planet Simple.

BUSINESS ON PLANET SIMPLE—
CONTROL AND EFFICIENCY

Planet Simple's assumptions of how the world works, combined with our innate propensity for spurious certitude, underpin today's business objectives of control and efficiency. Because we think we know the world, we assume we can control it. Because we assume equilibrium and stability, we can focus on efficiency.

Objectives of control and efficiency have their roots in the *scientific management* methods promulgated by American engineer Frederick Winslow Taylor in 1911.[32] Although *scientific* management gives Taylor's mindset an air of legitimacy, it was a reductionist view of science that failed many basic tests of the true scientific method.[33] It was born out of Planet Simple assumptions of how the world works, and so we may call it *Planet Simple management.*

As founder of the industrial efficiency movement, Taylor analyzed the production of pig iron in factories by breaking down the process into its component parts and determining standard levels of output for each job. His goal was to increase efficiency by standardizing and speeding up work on the factory floor to create mass production.

Specialization and standardization of tasks, recording and reporting of all activity, pecuniary carrots and sticks—these were the legacy of Taylor and his disciples for subsequent generations. Planet Simple management ideals of organizing factory production were increasingly adopted in a wide range of manufacturing industries in the interwar period. By the 1950s, they were the norm at companies like General Motors and are still in wide, if less obvious, practice today.

From humble beginnings, Planet Simple management "has worked its way into the fabric of all modern industrial societies, where it is now so common as to go unnoticed by most people."[34] Its dominance is buoyed by the belief that it can cure every problem affecting society if properly applied. At its core, Planet Simple management has visions of predictability and control over issues to which it is applied, subscribing to the myth that science and technology would not only increase resource use efficiency but control all unwanted variation as well. Uncertainty in nature is presumed to be replaced by certainty of human control.

Applying Planet Simple management assumes that a problem is well-bounded, clearly defined, relatively simple, and generally linear with respect to cause and effect. But when these management principles are applied to a complex, nonlinear, and poorly understood natural world, and when the same predictable outcomes are expected but rarely obtained, challenging ecological, social, and economic repercussions result. In fact, these strategies actually achieve the opposite by precipitating serious crises in human-natural systems—the ultimate trap of Planet Simple (as explained further in chapter 4).

Reality Bites Planet Simple

Recall Fukuyama's insight that there was never a period when humans existed as isolated individuals. We may add that there was never a period when humans existed separate to the natural environment.

Evidence of our interdependence with the natural world goes back to prehistoric and ancient times. The Epic of Gilgamesh (2700 BCE), considered one of the classical texts of antiquity, describes vast tracts of cedar forests in what is now southern Iraq. Gilgamesh defies the gods and cuts down the forest. In return, the gods curse Sumeria with fire (or possibly drought). By 2100 BCE, soil erosion and salt buildup had devastated agriculture.[35] Civilization moved north to Babylonia and Assyria. Again, deforestation became a factor in the rise and subsequent fall of these civilizations as well.[36]

Fast forwarding to more recent times, in the wake of the scientific and industrial revolutions of the seventeenth and eighteenth centuries, as we discussed above, humanity's influence on the environment became ever more obvious.

The negative results of Planet Simple thinking, underpinned by the biblical assumption of man's dominion over nature, only increased during the twentieth century. While the communist revolution in Russia in 1917 precipitated a new form of government—in opposition to the prevailing democratic and free-market model—it shared with its Western societies the same mindset regarding humanity's relationship with the natural world. As Russian revolutionary Leon Trotsky said: "The proper goal of communism is the domination of nature by technology and the domination of technology by planning, so that raw materials of nature will yield to mankind all that it needs and more besides."[37]

The end result, in both the East and West, has put humanity on a precarious footing. However, a counterrevolution was already afoot, one that had roots as early as the late nineteenth century and that has recently coalesced into the corporate sustainability movement. At its core, the movement asks us to question the Planet Simple mindset that still governs much of modern business management, whether we fully realize it or not. In the next chapter, we will turn to the increasing challenge presented to Planet Simple thinking, and the rise of today's corporate sustainability movement.

CHAPTER 2

Planet Simple's Meltdown

> *As we know, there are known knowns; there are things we know we know. We also know there are known unknowns; that is to say we know there are some things we do not know. But there are also unknown unknowns—the ones we don't know we don't know.*
>
> —Donald Rumsfeld

The Cracks Appear

Almost as early as the Industrial Revolution was developing around the world, alternative voices were emerging, starting to question Planet Simple thinking. One of the first in the United States was Vermont congressman George Perkins Marsh. In March 1847, he gave a speech to the Agricultural Society of Rutland County, Vermont. As the Library of Congress described the historic speech:

> This powerful address gave voice to ideas that would be a catalytic force in the movement to conserve America's natural resources. Marsh recognized the human capacity for destruction of the environment and advocated better management of resources and active efforts toward restoration of the land—innovative ideas for this period.[38]

Most environmental advocacy efforts of the nineteenth century in the United States were focused on two primary objectives. One was focused on obvious environmental disasters that impacted human health such as air pollution in urban areas or polluted waterways. The other objective was preserving America's natural habitat, a movement highlighted by the creation of the Sierra Club by John Muir in 1892.

These land conservation movements accelerated during the presidency of Theodore Roosevelt (1901–1909), who set aside 237 million acres of land for federal protection, a mark never since exceeded by any American president. Still, both Muir and Roosevelt had little sympathy for the native peoples who once inhabited these lands and largely viewed them as natural playgrounds for wealthy, white Americans, and often as still worthy of natural resource extraction. They also fell prey to Planet Simple assumptions of stability, assuming that it was possible and desirable to try to conserve natural areas "as they are" in perpetuity, a point we will revisit in Part II.

There were also concerns over social impacts of the Industrial Revolution. Upton Sinclair's 1906 book, *The Jungle*, exposed working conditions in the meatpacking plants of Chicago at the turn of the century.[39] In the form of a novel, *The Jungle* tells the story of working-class poverty, a lack of social support, harsh and unpleasant living and working conditions, and hopelessness among many workers. In contrast to these elements is the deeply rooted corruption of both corporate bosses and politicians. In a book review, the writer Jack London called it "the Uncle Tom's Cabin of wage slavery."[40]

Despite Sinclair's focus on working conditions, most readers were more concerned with passages from that book that exposed various health violations or unsanitary practices in the American meatpacking industry during the early twentieth century, including its impact on the environment. As Sinclair wrote in one passage, the smoke from the plants "came as if self-imperiled, driving all before it, a perpetual explosion. It was inexhaustible; one stared, waiting to see it stop, but still the great streams rolled out. They spread in vast clouds overhead, writhing, curling, then uniting in one giant river, they streamed away down the sky, stretching a black pall as far as the eye could reach."[41]

The book led to various reforms including the Meat Inspection Act and the Pure Food Act, which resulted in the creation of the Food and Drug Administration (FDA) in 1906.

An equally compelling and influential book was published a half century later by Rachel Carson in 1962, *Silent Spring*. Carson detailed the environmental harm caused by indiscriminate use of pesticides.[42] She also accused chemical companies of spreading disinformation and of public officials for accepting without question the marketing claims of pesticide producers.

Corporate criticism of the book was swift and brutal. Robert White-Stevens and Thomas Jukes, both biochemists at the now-defunct American Cyanamid Corporation, were two of the most aggressive critics, especially of Carson's analysis of the pesticide DDT. According to White-Stevens, "If man were to follow the teachings of Miss Carson, we would return to the Dark Ages, and the insects and diseases and vermin would once again inherit the earth."[43]

Many critics repeatedly said that Carson was arguing for the elimination of all pesticides, but she made it clear in her book that this was not her intention. Instead, she encouraged a more responsible use of pesticides combined with a greater appreciation for the chemicals' impact on ecosystems. Still, her work was groundbreaking for the time. Mark Hamilton Lytle, a professor of history and environmental studies at Bard College, wrote that Carson "quite self-consciously decided to write a book calling into question the paradigm of scientific progress that defined postwar American culture."[44]

Over the next sixty years, from the publication of *Silent Spring* in 1962 to the present day, the environmental would march forward, at times fitfully. This would be joined by the civil rights movement and the fight for racial justice. The two movements would often march two steps forward, one step back, but with a united sense that humanity's trajectory was straying from the aspirations of freedom and prosperity for all.

The publication of Rachel Carson's book coincided with a White House Conservation Conference, convened by President John F. Kennedy in May 1962. It was the first such conference since President Theodore Roosevelt's conference of governors in 1908, a convocation that was also inspired, in part, by the increased public awareness of environmental and worker rights issues perpetuated by *The Jungle*.

Six years later, the president's younger brother, Robert F. Kennedy, would prove to be one of the first national leaders to call for a more fulsome accounting of the nation's gross national product (GNP), one that considered factors far beyond industrial production and consumer consumption. Speaking from the campaign trail in 1968, and echoing a Planet Earth mentality, he stated:

> Too much and too long, we seem to have surrendered community excellence and community values in the

mere accumulation of material things. Our gross national product ... if we should judge America by that—counts air pollution and cigarette advertising and ambulances to clear our highways of carnage. It counts special locks for our doors and the jails for those who break them. It counts the destruction of our redwoods and the loss of our natural wonder in chaotic sprawl. It counts napalm and the cost of a nuclear warhead, and armored cars for police who fight riots in our streets. It counts Whitman's rifle and Speck's knife, and the television programs which glorify violence in order to sell toys to our children. Yet the gross national product does not allow for the health of our children, the quality of their education, or the joy of their play. It does not include the beauty of our poetry or the strength of our marriages; the intelligence of our public debate or the integrity of our public officials. It measures neither our wit nor our courage; neither our wisdom nor our learning; neither our compassion nor our devotion to our country; it measures everything, in short, except that which makes life worthwhile. And it tells us everything about America except why we are proud that we are Americans.[45]

Despite Robert Kennedy's call for a more fulsome measurement of the country's GNP, one that would factor in a multitude of externalities, there were already voices among the neoconservative movement advocating for a far different approach.

In 1970, just two years after Robert Kennedy had been assassinated on the campaign trail, not long after delivering the speech above, Milton Friedman was penning his editorial in the *New York Times*, which we discussed above, advocating for the Friedman Doctrine—

putting profits as the sole objective of business without regard for social consequences.[46]

Many large corporations, however, recognized that many of its customers, and even its employees, were increasingly concerned with environmental and societal issues, and that their companies needed to signal that they were not to blame. This brings us to the first Planet Simple trap of the book.

Planet Simple Trap: Corporate Social Responsibility

Planet Simple traps refer to ways that corporate sustainability has been distorted by the prevailing Planet Simple mindset. These traps allow for practitioners to—knowingly or not—claim that they are implementing sustainability while failing to address the underlying Planet Simple assumptions that gave rise to today's challenges in the first place.

The 1970s saw the birth of the corporate social responsibility (CSR) movement, a glaring Planet Simple trap that still pervades today's traditional business models. The name itself gives it away. Embedded in the name is the assumption that business is irresponsible and needs a cleanup strategy to balance it out. While this assumption may have made sense at the time, it is jarring to most businesses today. If your business is already responsible, why do you need a responsibility strategy?

CSR often involves philanthropy, which includes activities like making donations to nonprofits, coordinating employee volunteering, or engaging in activity with community initiatives. The PR or brand building benefit of these activities is usually quite high. Many companies remain of the view that corporate sustainability is CSR, philanthropy, where the PR value is high but the impact on internal operations of the firm or its outside impact is less clear. Many, more primitive CSR efforts are "end-of-pipe" solutions, in other words more focused on the problem as opposed to the root causes of the problem. These efforts seek to "balance" corporate impacts and assume that the wider harms are localized, reversible, and restricted to bad actors, rather than being systemic.

CSR is a significant Planet Simple trap facing the corporate sustainability movement today. It results in the wider public viewing sustainability as separate to "core business," as more of a charity initiative than a legitimate strategic imperative. As a result, businesses think they have *achieved* sustainability without ever transforming the business model.

- -

Planet Simple's Boss Battle

Blockbuster movies, epic novels, and all-the-rage video games almost always feature the hero systematically defeating (or somehow avoiding) salvos of obstacles as part of a harrowing adventure to reach the "boss battle"—an all-encompassing opponent that often requires a special trick or a targetable weak point to exploit and ultimately save the day. Think Frodo Baggins facing down orcs, trolls, and Ringwraiths before finally defeating the Dark Lord Sauron. Or Homer's *The Iliad* and the dramatic one-on-one battle between Achilles and Hector.

As Planet Simple prevailed over criticism of its impact on things that people can "see"—like clean air, clean water, and natural forests—a few savvy scientists began to investigate the impact of things they could not see. As early as 1856, Eunice Newton Foote demonstrated that carbon dioxide (CO_2)—produced by the burning of fossil fuels such as wood, coal, or fuel oil—is a greenhouse gas (GHG) and suggested that if the atmosphere continued to accumulate CO_2, it would lead to a warmer Earth.[47] According to historian John Perlin at the University of California, Santa Barbara, Foote is likely the first scientist to recognize the potential for human-induced climate change.[48]

Nearly two centuries, billions of new humans, and gigatons of GHG emissions later, climate change has come to be Planet Simple's boss battle. Rather than the battle being localized and outside the purview of traditional business, climate change came to be seen as a systemic result of our collective actions: something that is now acknowledged to be a significant financial, economic, and existential threat. If we had known 150 years ago that our present situation would occur, I believe people would have thought and acted differently. But we didn't. We assumed (still do) that we are separate from the environment and that things like pollution would just evaporate and everything would balance out. Manifest Destiny was an invitation to go forth and conquer, implicitly assuming there would be no long-term consequences.

Climate change is the ultimate unknown unknown, an unintended consequence of Planet Simple assumptions, and a boss battle for which there is no special trick or targetable weak point. It is an emergent outcome that is greater than the sum of its parts—turning Planet Simple reductionism on its head.

A changing climate also upsets the Planet Simple assumptions of stability and individualism. No longer can we assume that human or corporate behavior, if acting within the law or rules, can function on its own without considerations for its broader impact on society or the environment. In short, climate change is undeniable proof that we are not on Planet Simple.

Just like Ptolemaic astronomy served humanity well for a while, so Planet Simple served humanity well while our impacts were localized. But now, for the first time *ever*, we are a global species. Humans have now *scaled up* to be drivers of global change, a shift in spatial and temporal scale for which Planet Simple is not well-suited. As Gunderson, Allen, and Garmestani write in *Applied Panarchy*, "At the scale of the planet, human interventions of technology, fossil fuels, and global economies have altered self-organized biogeochemical cycles to the extent that we now live on a human-dominated planet in a phase of Earth's existence called the Anthropocene."[49] We will revisit the importance of scale for managing on Planet Earth in Part II.

The Rise of Stakeholder Capitalism

As climate change plunged the Planet Simple mindset into crisis, business institutions have tried to articulate alternative visions for how business can acknowledge the reality of Planet Earth. One such alternative, stakeholder capitalism, attempts to revisit the Planet Simple assumption that business exists separate from the world around it. It holds that a business cannot create long-term value for its shareholders without considering the interests of its stakeholders—customers, employees, communities, and the natural environment.[50] Stakeholder capitalism tries to acknowledge something that has been true all along: that a business depends on natural, human, and other social resources and relationships to create value.

In their 2021 book, *Talent, Strategy, Risk*, authors Bill McNabb, Ram Charan, and Dennis Carey argue that stakeholder capitalism can lead to greater long-term value for the enterprise. "Investors often view social benefits as contrary to financial results—that initiating, say, a zero-carbon strategy will mean higher costs and lower profits. In the short run, that may be true. But such a focus can deliver long-term gains; from future savings and the creation of new lines of business, and from the higher value people will increasingly place on companies that pursue such goals."[51]

In 2019, the Business Roundtable, a Washington, DC–based nonprofit group that includes the CEOs of many large American corporations, made headlines around the world when it redefined the purpose of a corporation to be squarely in line with the goals of stakeholder capitalism. And in late 2019, Klaus Schwab, the founder and chairman of the World Economic Forum, issued his 2020 Davos Manifesto—The Universal Purpose of a Company in the Fourth Industrial Revolution—which states:

> The purpose of a company is to engage all its stakehold-
> ers in shared and sustained value creation. In creating such
> value, a company serves not only its shareholders, but all its
> stakeholders—employees, customers, suppliers, local com-
> munities and society at large. The best way to understand
> and harmonize the divergent interests of all stakeholders is
> through a shared commitment to policies and decisions that
> strengthen the long-term prosperity of a company.[52]

From Efficiency to Resilience

Once the Planet Simple assumptions of stability and equilibrium fail, the business objective of efficiency must fall too.

When you assume simplicity, you assume stability, predictability, and control. You assume the future will be the same as the past; as such, you can manage for efficiency, the key driver of business. However, once you debunk Planet Simple, you realize you can't predict the future. You need to think long term because managing only for efficiency becomes potentially catastrophic.

After the 2015 Paris Agreement committed investors to direct their capital flows consistent with the investment needed to stop global warming, a group of economists led by Michael Bloomberg set out to refocus the priorities of business. Bloomberg led the establishment of the Task Force on Climate-related Financial Disclosures (TCFD) under the oversight of the G20 Financial Stability Board (FSB).

The TCFD acknowledged the need for a new mindset when it recommended that businesses disclose their *resilience* to climate change. As we will explore in this book, this is a fundamental departure from the traditional focus on efficiency.

The International Sustainability Standards Board (ISSB) has further cemented the importance of resilience thinking across business, encouraging companies to disclose its resilience to any of its significant environmental and social issues, thus acknowledging that climate change is just one of the sustainability-related factors that business must address as it seeks to create long-term value.

This book's central argument, as will be spelled out in subsequent chapters, is that managing for resilience is fundamentally incompatible with today's business mindset (Planet Simple). No amount of assessment, scenario analysis, or reporting will achieve resilience if we remain wedded to a Planet Simple assumption of how the world works. Instead, it will become distorted into more of the same.

Before we turn to understanding the reality of Planet Earth, we will turn our attention to one of the most significant Planet Simple distortions—the ESG investing movement that spiked in the years since the Paris Agreement. A deeper dive into ESG investing will help contrast it with fundamental mindset shift outlined in Parts II and III.

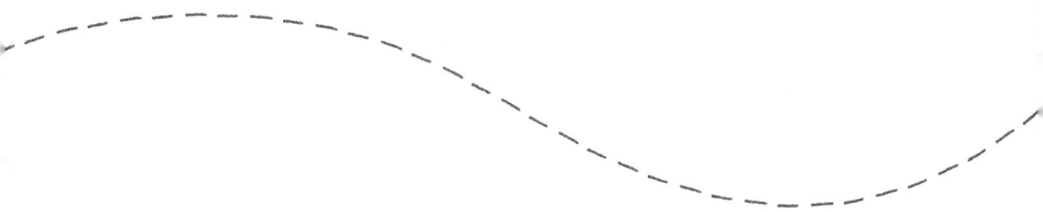

CHAPTER 3

Planet Simple's Hammer

> *If the only tool you have is a hammer, it is tempting to treat everything as if it were a nail.*
>
> —Abraham Maslow

People are generally resistant to change, whether it's adopting an industry-changing business model or taking a different route to work. Corporate sustainability faces the same challenge. When investors first recognized the need to consider sustainability, instead of approaching it as a fundamentally different track to success, they held true to prevailing Planet Simple thinking that sustainability was a discrete, separate factor to be integrated into their existing analyses. Unsurprisingly, that hasn't worked as planned.

The whole point of corporate sustainability is understanding the *connection* between environment, society, and business. If your discipline has long assumed that environmental and social factors are not important, that financial factors are the complete picture, then corporate sustainability is a fundamental paradigm shift. As

Kuhn states, people don't deal with such a challenge by changing their mindset. Instead, they try to distort the new reality to fit their existing methods.

So it is with ESG investing, which has been in the firing line in recent years and for good reason. It doesn't fundamentally address the systemic challenges and assumptions that got us here in the first place. The ESG investing movement is important to cover because of its visibility and also because it represents the most high-profile example of trying to fit the challenge of sustainability into the "inflexible box that the [traditional] paradigm supplies."[53]

The Birth of ESG

It's not surprising that many equate corporate sustainability with ESG investing because, in some ways, this is where it all started. While ESG investing can find its roots in the socially responsible investing movement of the 1960s and 1970s, ESG was first coined as a term in 2005.

The previous year, in 2004, the former UN Secretary General Kofi Annan wrote a letter to fifty CEOs of major financial institutions, asking them to participate in a joint initiative between the UN Global Compact, the International Finance Corporation (IFC), and the Swiss government. The goal of the initiative, he explained, was to find ways to integrate ESG factors into the world's capital markets.

A year later, the initiative published its landmark study, "Who Cares Wins."[54] The report made the argument, novel at the time, that embedding ESG factors into capital markets was good for business, good for the markets, and good for the environment and society.

Around 2013–2014, however, attitudes began to shift as more evidence accumulated that incorporating ESG factors into a business led to improved profits and stock market performance. One of the most influential studies was completed by three business school professors: George Serafeim, Bob Eccles, and Ioannis Ioannou. The study was titled, "The Impact of Corporate Sustainability on Organizational Processes and Performance Management."[55]

After evaluating 180 companies for the period from 1993 to 2009, the authors conclude: "We provide evidence that High Sustainability companies significantly outperform their counterparts over the long-term, both in terms of stock market as well as accounting performance."[56] This was big news and showed that companies that had truly incorporated sustainability into their business processes, as opposed to the Planet Simple trap of CSR described in chapter 1, had a positive effect on what CEOs and investors care about the most: stock market performance.

Wall Street Co-opts ESG

Despite these positive early developments that focused on ESG as a recognition of the *connection* between environment, society, and business, ESG was soon co-opted by the investment products and solutions machine of Wall Street. Their collective assessment was: ESG sells. Or, more specifically, ESG funds sell. Big money managers got in on the game from Blackrock to Fidelity to Vanguard. Money poured into "socially responsible" exchange-traded funds (ETFs) and mutual funds and often at much higher fees than traditional index funds. The ESG gravy train was moving forward on full steam ahead.

And then came August 2021, a bad month for ESG investing. In that month, two whistleblowers emerged: insiders who had witnessed how the ESG fund sausage was made and marketed to retail investors.

The first was Tariq Fancy, the former chief investment officer for sustainable investing at Blackrock, the world's largest money manager with nearly $10 trillion in assets under management. The firm's founder, Larry Fink, had been an early proponent of incorporating ESG into investment decision-making. His 2018 letter to CEOs was titled "A Sense of Purpose"[57] and cautioned CEOs that if they did not adopt sustainable practices into their companies, they would no longer receive the support, or investment, from Blackrock.

Fancy published his "Secret Diary of a Sustainable Investor" in August 2021.[58] It had three parts and was followed up by an epilogue in June 2022.[59] In total, the pieces run to over thirty thousand words. His first argument, which might have been obvious to any savvy investor, was that ESG funds had little to no impact on society or the environment for the simple fact that even "dirty" companies will be bid up by investors because they still produce profits and stock market returns.[60]

In the end, concluded Fancy, ESG funds make socially conscious investors feel better about their investment, but really don't change anything. Fancy also commented on the Planet Simple mindset that governs ESG fund marketing. In talking about Blackrock marketing execs, he wrote, "They made clear their view: the key to selling the product was to keep it simple, even if that meant glossing over how it directly contributed to fighting climate change, which was always hard to explain and at best a bit uncertain."[61] Clearly, Fancy's colleagues had employed the tried-and-true KISS method: Keep it (Planet) Simple Stupid.

With trillions flowing into ESG-related funds, a whole cottage industry emerged, in terms of rating agencies, academic studies, think tanks, conferences, and so on. In his Secret Diary, Fancy would find many of them in his crosshairs. One item he took issue with was ESG ratings, which was often encapsulated into single "ESG score," meant to reflect everything a company was doing in terms of the environment, society, and corporate governance. Fancy says this is almost impossible. "Often, everything ranging from levels of greenhouse gas emissions to supply chain labor standards and the diversity of the board of directors is mashed into a single 'ESG score' for a company, which serves as a quick and convenient measure of corporate virtue."[62]

In the end, Fancy left Blackrock, ultimately concluding that "trying to create real-world social impact through sustainable investing felt like pushing on a string."[63] Instead, he called for a much broader remake of the "rules of the game," arguing that voluntary commitments won't work and that more fundamental policy changes were needed such as a carbon tax that would be applied universally.[64]

In the same month, August 2021, another whistleblower emerged, Desiree Fixler, the head of sustainability at Deutsche Bank's money-management arm, DWS. In its 2020 annual report published in March 2021, the German money-management behemoth claimed that over half of its $540 billion of assets under management was graded according to ESG criteria. It further stated that, "As a firm, we have placed ESG at the heart of everything that we do."[65]

But Fixler, working from the inside and tasked with spearheading the firm's sustainability efforts, found something quite different. According to the *Wall Street Journal*, she made a presentation to the Executive Board where she pointed out that "the firm had no clear ambition or strategy, lacked policies on coal and other topics and that ESG teams were seen as specialists rather than being an integral part of the decision-making."[66]

Turning to the often-ignored issue of governance in the ESG ratings world, Fixler, for example, could not understand how the German payment processing company, Wirecard, had a business ethics score of "B," the second highest rating. The fintech darling collapsed spectacularly in June 2020 when a $2 billion hole was found in its finances.[67] And yet its DWS rating was still "B." Fraud can be hard to spot, for sure, but in this case there were warning signs. As far back as 2019, the *Financial Times* ran a series of articles on the company that "aired allegations of accounting fraud, falsification of documents and money laundering,"[68] according to the *Wall Street Journal*. This led the company to hire an outside auditor, who two months before the firm collapsed released a report saying that it could not verify existence of the firm's cash. And yet, at DWS, the firm's ESG score remained at the second highest rating. In July, after the firm had collapsed, DWS dropped it to F.[69]

The day before DWS's annual report was published in March 2021, Desiree Fixler was fired. She soon went public with her story, arguing that "posturing with big statements on climate action and inclusion without the goods to back it up is really quite harmful as it prevents money and action from flowing to the right place."[70]

Before too long, DWS was raided by German federal police, and the firm was found to have misrepresented its ESG initiatives by a wide margin. Many senior executives were fired including the firm's CEO, COO, CIO, and head of communications. The firm has now revamped its ESG strategy and policies and has committed to reform.

But the damage was done, providing more ammunition for the many ESG critics, who claim it is just another example of "woke capitalism." Still, the hits for ESG investing just kept on coming.

In January 2022, the *Wall Street Journal*'s Streetwise column published a series of articles on ESG investing under the headline, "Why the Sustainable Investment Craze Is Flawed."[71] The writer's arguments echoed Fancy's in that even with the huge inflows of investment dollars into ESG funds, it was having little impact on either the environment or society.[72] The articles also pointed out that ESG funds come at much higher fees than traditional index funds and yet are often simply "closet indexers," comprised of portfolios that differ little from the much lower-cost index funds.[73]

Seeing Through the Hype Cycle

Although ESG investing failed to live up to the expectations that some had for it to save the day, it is yet another signal that a fundamental shift from Planet Simple to Planet Earth is underway. For centuries, investors ignored environmental and social considerations because on Planet Simple, they don't matter. On the back of calls to acknowledge the reality that climate change is a financial risk, they tried to force that reality into their existing methods. As Derek Brower, former energy editor at the *Financial Times*, eloquently put it in June 2023: "This isn't a task for your favorite ESG-focused portfolio manager or the tech bros."[74]

Looking through the lens of Planet Simple, we can more clearly see failures of ESG investing across three themes:

- Assumptions of measurability—Assuming that analysts can evaluate something like "climate" with enough certainty to provide useful information for decision-making.

Analysts' models require numbers to arrive at decisive scores they can sell to decision-makers, so they try to tweak the messy reality of sustainability to fit their neat method, rather than attempting the disorderly (but more accurate) work of changing their existing method to fit the reality of sustainability.

- Assumptions of isolation—ESG investing often considers sustainability factors as distinct risks (scores) to be analyzed alongside other financial factors.

In reality, environmental and social factors should be considered as drivers of performance rather than standalone factors. The consideration of ESG factors *alongside* financial factors (as opposed to considering ESG factors as the broader context for financial performance) also represents the flattening of scale that will be discussed further in chapter 4.

- Assumptions of novelty—ESG investing saw sustainability as a new "product" to be sold to address the latest "trend."

This fails to recognize that environmental and social factors have influenced financial performance since the beginning of time. It is far easier to try to bolt on something new than to revisit the assumptions upon which the entire field of investment analysis is founded.

The Gartner hype cycle is useful to further explain how ESG investing, despite its shortcomings, signals the underlying mindset shift underway in business today.[75] Developed to explain hype and eventual adoption of technology, this concept also handily represents what is currently going on in the corporate sustainability space. The Gartner hype cycle comprises five phases:[76]

1. Innovation trigger

2. Peak of inflated expectations

3. Trough of disillusionment

4. Slope of enlightenment

5. Plateau of productivity

Looking at this from a sustainability perspective, if we consider corporate sustainability to have arrived on the scene around 2000, then we may see superficial attempts at CSR and ESG investing mania as the *peak of inflated expectations*—companies could "do good" without affecting their core business and investors could rush in to save the day without upsetting their fundamentals.

As time passes, people learn more about the underlying challenge. A lot of people who rushed in now realize they are in too deep and try to back out. These "failures" are taken to be disillusionment with the original idea (corporate sustainability) and politicians and the anti-ESG movement swarm in to try to stamp it out once and for all (because they recognize the fundamental threat that the reality of sustainability poses). This is the trough of disillusionment, and we are probably at this point in the corporate sustainability hype cycle at the time of writing (the year 2024).

What my work, and this book, tries to do is help us all see through the noise of ESG investing, anti-ESG and so on, so we can see the underlying reality that corporate sustainability is trying to address. I am attempting to speed up the Slope of Enlightenment so we can get to the Plateau of Productivity, to Planet Earth, which is when we all realize that corporate sustainability is not charity, it is not ESG investing, and it is not a sham. Rather, it is a wake-up call to the reality that business is, always has been, and always will be part of a wider environmental and social context.

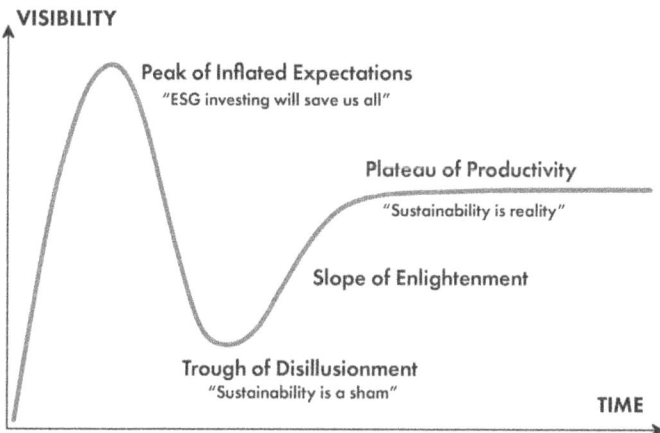

VISIBILITY

Peak of Inflated Expectations
"ESG investing will save us all"

Plateau of Productivity
"Sustainability is reality"

Slope of Enlightenment

Trough of Disillusionment
"Sustainability is a sham"

TIME

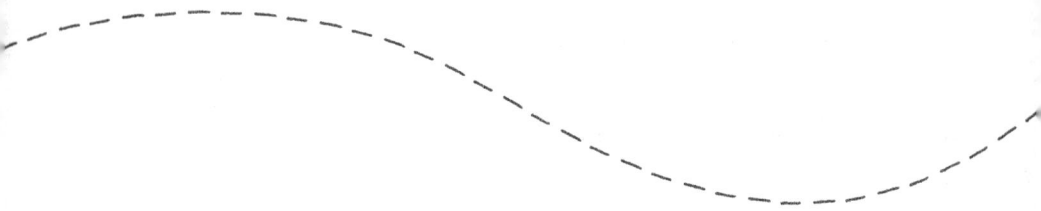

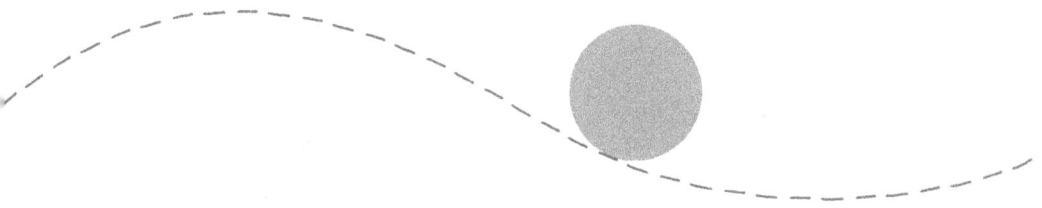

PART II:

Planet Earth

Where there is danger, that which will save us also grows.

—Friedrich Holderlin (1770–1843)

Having introduced the prevalence of Planet Simple in Part I, we now turn to unpack a revolution in the scientific understanding of how Planet Earth works, and its implications for business practice. The reality is that for any business organization to truly manage for resilience, it needs to revisit the Planet Simple mindset and replace it with today's understanding of how things work on Planet Earth. This understanding has been established by resilience science over the last fifty years. This is what we will cover in chapter 4, where we will establish the connection between resilience science and our understanding of Planet Earth. We will then turn to the implications of resilience science for corporate strategy and decision-making in chapters 5 and 6.

It goes without saying that I will need to be selective in condensing topics so vast, each of which would not be considered too great for a whole lifetime of research, into a sequence of short chapters. My objective is not to provide an exhaustive review and I will offer many citations to direct an interested reader to supporting work. Instead, my objective is to demonstrate how the main conclusions of this book—the need for business to move from Planet Simple to Planet Earth—is founded upon a coherent body of research based on empirical evidence and spanning several disciplines.

CHAPTER 4

Resilience Science 101

Resilience science has been successful because it quite simply describes reality better than previous scientific worldviews.

—Lance H. Gunderson, Craig R. Allen, and Ahjond Garmestani,

Applied Panarchy

The corporate sustainability movement has led to calls for business to focus on resilience. But what does resilience actually mean?

Today's interest in resilience is linked to advances in our understanding of how the world works that began around fifty years ago. In 1973, Canadian ecologist C. S. "Buzz" Holling published *Resilience and Stability in Ecological Systems*,[77] a seminal paper that has been cited more than twenty-one thousand times since (about once a day on average for the last fifty years).

At the time of Holling's work, the natural sciences worked within a Planet Simple mindset, often excluding humans from studies and treating human actions as external to natural systems. Holling's work spawned the discipline of resilience science, which holds that human and natural systems cannot be understood in isolation. Instead, resilience science defined the "social-ecological system" as the appropriate unit of analysis (which I refer to throughout this book as "human-natural systems").[78]

Human-natural systems are neither humans embedded in natural systems nor ecosystems embedded in human systems, but a different entity altogether.[79] The reductionism of Planet Simple considers humans separate to natural and other systems, and in doing so overlooks important interdependencies and feedbacks between nature and society.[80] Not only do humans depend on natural systems for survival, but human influence on natural systems occurs at all scales and has become planetary, as indicated by human-caused climate change.[81] We will return to how resilience science explains human-induced climate change later in this chapter.

This chapter will step through the science behind these conclusions, to provide the empirical foundation for why Planet Simple management must change to better fit the reality of Planet Earth. Human beings, companies, governments, agricultural lands, national parks, cities, and the Earth itself are examples of human-natural systems at different scales (I will come back to the importance of scale later in this chapter). Resilience science has demonstrated that these systems have *emergent* properties that cannot be predicted through the analysis of their components in isolation. Planet Simple reductionism won't work. On Planet Earth, the whole is greater than the sum of its parts, refuting the Planet Simple assumption that individuals maximizing their self-interest would lead to the best interests of society at large (the "invisible hand"). Here, human-natural systems aren't S-I-M-P-L-E. Instead, we live in a world of constant change, defined by tipping points and true complexity[82]—as the ancient Greeks said, *change is the only constant.*

Revisiting the Importance of Mindset

A central argument in this book, introduced in chapter 1, is that business practice is based on a Planet Simple mindset (or *paradigm* per Kuhn in *Structure*). Trying to apply sustainability and resilience practice to business without shifting the mindset will not work, because the Planet Simple mindset will distort the meaning and intent of sustainability such that the initiatives fail to achieve their transformational objectives. The Planet Simple traps described throughout the book are examples of this distortion in play..

But first, let's revisit what we mean by *mindset*. Holling noted that "Humans collectively interact and make decisions based on constructs or ideas that are oversimplifications of a much more complex reality."[83] Kahneman echoed this in a more contemporary sense, as he demonstrated how the reality of human behavior often went against classical economic assumptions. According to Kahneman, our illusions "reduce the anxiety that we would experience if we allowed ourselves to fully acknowledge the uncertainties of existence."[84]

Our mindset is the set of assumptions we make about how the world works. We once thought the world was flat. We once thought the sun revolved around the Earth. We lived our lives according to these assumptions and no one thought too much about it until the incongruency of our experience combined with new mindset that better matched reality.

We are not always aware of the assumptions we are making. A function of philosophy is to challenge ideas that appear obvious but that may be fundamentally mistaken. This book argues that business's current mindset—Planet Simple—is fundamentally mistaken, and it offers an alternative mindset based on empirical research about the reality of Planet Earth. In this way, the philosophy of the book is less about abstraction (as philosophy today is commonly understood) and more about challenging how we think and make decisions through research grounded in real-world observation.

Nature Balanced, Nature Varied, and Nature Evolving

To help make our journey from Planet Simple to Planet Earth more accessible, I will step through different *caricatures of nature*. These are visualizations that illustrate different worldviews of reality held by people.

The caricature of nature resembling the Planet Simple mindset is Nature Balanced.[85] Nature Balanced is a view of human-natural systems existing at or near an equilibrium condition. If nature is disturbed, it will return to an equilibrium through (in systems terms) negative feedback. Nature appears to be infinitely forgiving. It is the myth of *maximum sustainable yield* and of achieving fixed carrying capacities for animals and humanity (we will revisit maximum sustainable yield later in the chapter). The mindset of Nature Balanced makes us think these targets are viable, but they end up imposing a static goal on a dynamic system.

Figure 1 displays a ball-in-basin diagram for Nature Balanced. Ball-in-basin diagrams are an established method for communicating complexity and will help illustrate the key mindset shifts on our journey from Planet Simple to Planet Earth. In ball-in-basin diagrams, the ball represents the current system state as defined by levels of component variables. The basins represent *basins of attraction*, or equilibrium configurations to which the system will tend to gravitate. The diagram suggests that if undisturbed, a system (the ball) will naturally progress over time to resemble the system conditions represented by the nadir, or "attractor," of its given basin.[86]

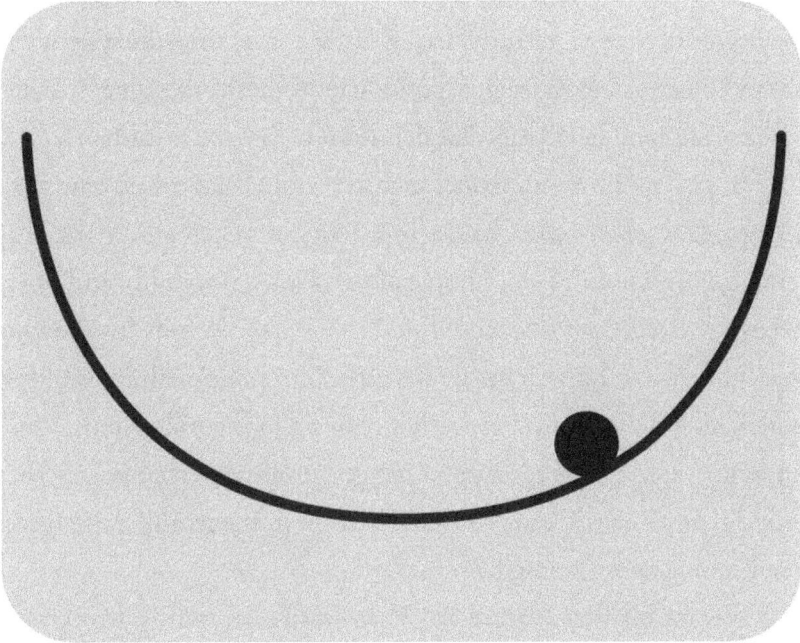

Figure 1. Ball-in-basin diagram for the Nature Balanced worldview. According to Nature Balanced, there is a single equilibrium (represented by the single basin) to which natural systems will gravitate regardless of the initial configuration. Any management action or other perturbation to the system is "balanced" by a tendency—assumed to be inherent to the system—to return to the equilibrium position.

Since Nature Balanced assumes systems gravitate toward a single equilibrium, its ball-in-basin diagram features a single basin (Figure 1). Nature appears "infinitely forgiving" because no matter how human actions alter system configurations (i.e., the position of the ball within the basin), Nature Balanced assumes the system will eventually and always gravitate toward this one equilibrium state.

When using ball-in-basin diagrams, system resilience may be conceptualized as the width at the top of the basin.[87] According to Nature Balanced, therefore, nature is infinitely resilient. Regardless of the degree of change, disturbance, or distress, over time the system will always come back to its original position by assuming the same structure, interactions, and feedbacks that defined it before the disturbance.

Single-equilibrium theories such as Nature Balanced assume stasis and *gradual, predictable* change in ecological systems over the long term, giving rise to Planet Simple assumptions of stability and linear behavior. Resilience science refuted these assumptions by showing that human-natural systems are dynamic (not static), exhibit multiple potential equilibrium states (rather than a single equilibrium),[88] and undergo rapid, unpredictable change (nonlinear change).[89] They found that while there are forces of balance in the world, these forces "can become overwhelmed."[90]

This meant that Nature Balanced wasn't necessarily wrong, but it was incomplete. To improve on Nature Balanced, we may consider the worldview of Nature Varied (see Figure 2).[91]

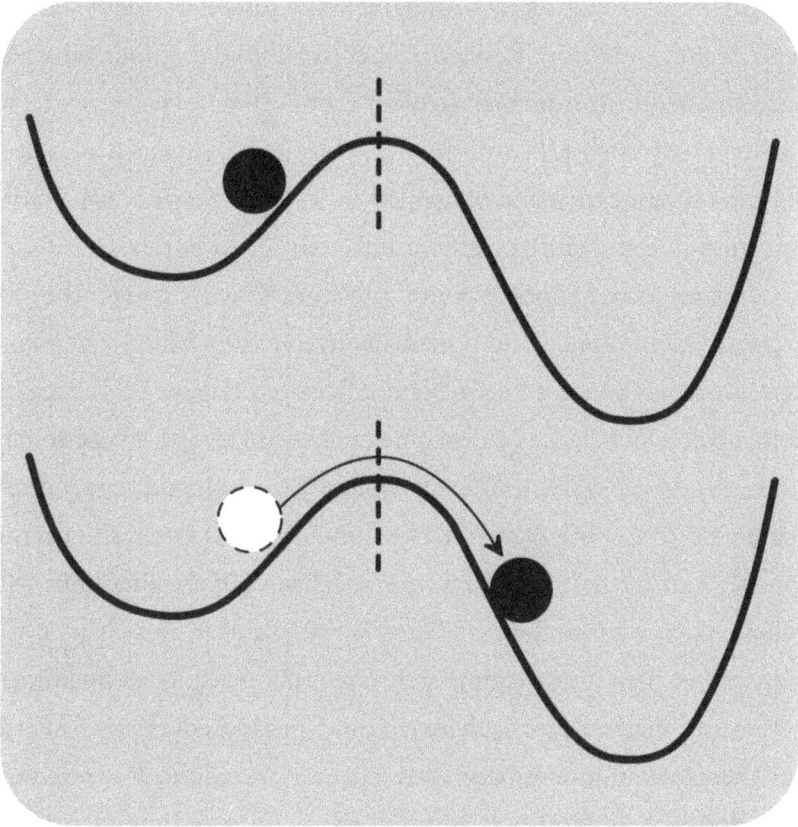

Figure 2. Ball-in-basin diagram for the Nature Varied worldview. According to Nature Varied, natural systems may gravitate toward multiple equilibria, depending on the initial conditions. Of importance is that disturbance resulting from climate change, extreme events, or management action may cause the system to cross a threshold (dotted line) such that it does not gravitate toward the equilibrium conditions that governed the system before the disturbance.

Nature Varied builds on Nature Balanced by introducing multiple possible equilibria (basins) for a given system. Its ball-in-basin diagram features a stability landscape with two or more basins (Figure 2), reflecting the reality that systems may cross a threshold, or tipping point, resulting in a fundamentally different system state or equilibrium condition. Resilience scientists found that following perturbation resulting from management action, climate change, extreme natural events such as fires or floods, or business events such as radical shift in consumer demand or regulation, a system may not necessarily return to its pre-disturbance state automatically over time.

The presence of tipping points in Nature Varied allows for the conceptualization of rapid and potentially irreversible change—an inconceivable outcome according to Nature Balanced (Figure 1). The reality is that forces of balance can become overwhelmed, and a system may undergo a *regime shift* to a different equilibrium set of conditions.[92] Such regime shifts have been described for human-natural systems across the globe,[93] and further insight into the mechanics of a regime shift will follow when we introduce the *adaptive cycle* later in this chapter. Of importance here is that regime shifts are often precipitated by human action and are associated with loss of function or productivity.[94] Worse yet, these human-induced degraded states are often difficult to reverse.[95]

Resilience scientists have implored us to take note of tipping points and regime shifts because of the potential for unimaginably costly and irreversible change. In 2018, researchers tracking increases in GHG emissions issued a contemporary warning of crossing global tipping points that would cause continued warming on a "Hothouse Earth" pathway even if humans are able to reduce GHG emissions into the future.[96] Crossing the tipping point would be effectively irreversible, and the resulting trajectory would likely cause serious disruptions to ecosystems, society, and economies.

Although the addition of tipping points and regime shifts paints a more comprehensive picture than Nature Balanced, Nature Varied is also incomplete. The problem is that Nature Varied presumes an unchanging stability landscape where the contours of the basins are fixed over time.

To accommodate the possibility of changes to underlying stability land-scapes, we may consider the worldview of Nature Evolving (Figure 3).

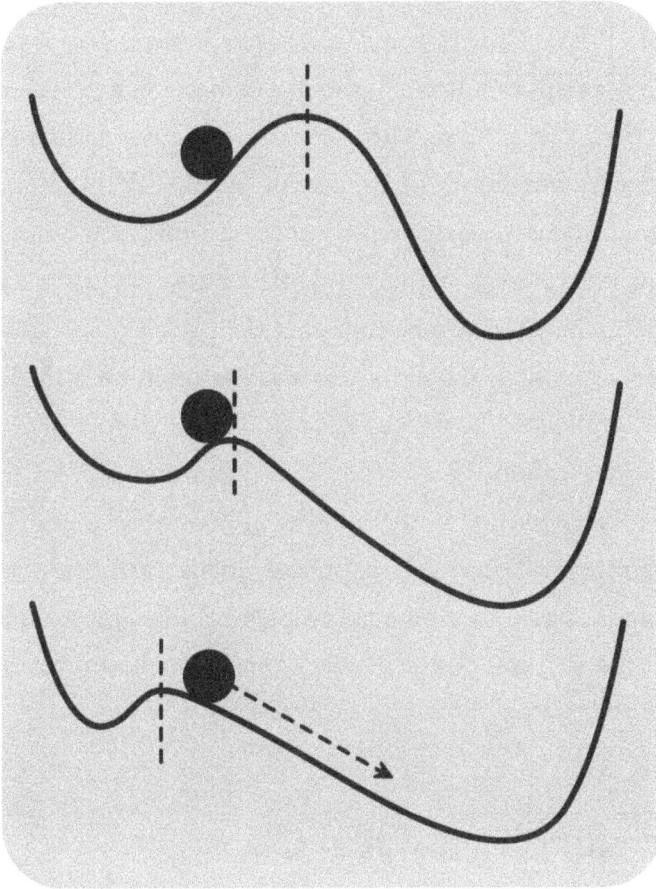

Figure 3. Ball-in-basin diagram for the Nature Evolving worldview. Nature Evolving assumes the existence of multiple equilibria and potential changes to the underlying stability landscape. Changes to stability landscapes alter the resilience of equilibrium states; such systems may find themselves closer to thresholds or even within another basin entirely despite management succeeding in holding system components constant (as illustrated by the ball remaining in the same position, but ending up in a different basin of attraction because of underlying changes to the stability landscape).

Nature Evolving is a view of an actively shifting stability landscape with self-organization.[97] Self-organization refers to the idea that while the stability landscape (i.e., the contours of the basins) affects the behavior of system components (i.e., the ball), these components, as well as exogenous events such as global climate change and management action, affect the stability landscape. Human-natural systems, therefore, are moving targets, evolving because of the impacts of management action, expansion of human societies, and other factors such as climate change.[98] These and other *drivers of change* may alter a system's stability landscape such that the system traces closer to a threshold or perhaps transitions to another basin even though the system components themselves remain constant (Figure 3).[99]

The implications of a Nature Evolving worldview for management typically couched in the mindset of Nature Balanced (i.e., the Planet Simple mindset) are significant. In fact, we could say that management based around static, single-equilibrium assumptions leads to the *ultimate trap of Planet Simple* (which will be revisited later in this chapter).

Understanding System Change: The Adaptive Cycle

Because resilience science prioritizes systems analysis over reductionism, it offers insights that are directly applicable to real-world complexity. The adaptive cycle is one such insight.

The adaptive cycle was developed to provide a model of system change that reflected real-world behavior observed by resilience scientists. Sometimes system change is slow (think of the gradual accumulation of plant biomass or corporate wealth), sometimes it is fast (a forest fire or a market crash). There are also periods of stability interspersed with periods of instability (pandemics and political elections or coups). Some changes give rise to novelty, while others result in more of the same. The adaptive cycle brings this all together and has proven to be a valid means of understanding change in political regimes, local and national economies, and other human-natural systems.[100]

Referring back to the ball-in-basin diagrams, we may think of the adaptive cycle as describing the change that occurs within the ball as it moves along the basin contours. The adaptive cycle suggests that systems exhibit four distinct and usually sequential phases of change. The phases of the adaptive cycle are presented in the following table, in their original terminology and with an analog nomenclature that we will use to apply the framework to business management.

PHASES OF THE ADAPTIVE CYCLE

Human-Natural Systems	Business Analogy	Description
Exploitation	Growth	Buildup of structures, capital, and connections with the system. Rapid entry, growth, and colonization of recently disturbed or otherwise vacant areas, markets, niches.
Conservation	Production	System structure reaches a climax state with a high degree of connectivity, efficiency, and stability that allows for maximum productivity.
Release	Destruction	System structure breaks down, usually as a result of disturbance from within or external to the system—resulting in a rapid loss of connectedness and productivity.
Reorganization	Renewal	The loss of connectedness opens up opportunities for new species, participants, and ideas to enter the system, and sets the stage for the next cycle of growth.

Each phase corresponds to a unique combination of *connectedness* between system components (x-axis) and *productivity* (y-axis). When describing the adaptive cycle, the *front loop* is the procession from lower left to upper right, or from growth to production, and the *back loop* is the procession from lower right to upper left, or from destruction to renewal (Figure 4).

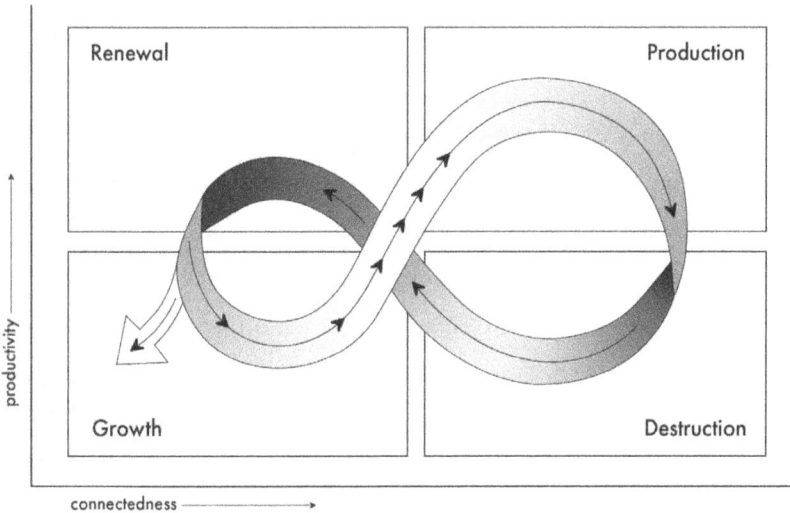

Figure 4. The adaptive cycle offers a framework for explaining how systems progress through sequential stages of productivity and connectedness.

A system's journey on the adaptive cycle begins with the front loop, starting at the bottom-left of the adaptive cycle. The system enjoys a period of growth, fueled by inputs of energy and resources, resulting in the accumulation of structures, capital, and connections within the system. The growth phase emphasizes rapid colonization of recently disturbed or otherwise vacant areas. The system's increase in connectedness (x-axis) allows for an increase in productivity (y-axis) and is why the front loop moves from the bottom-left to the top-right of the adaptive cycle.

The system enters the production phase, featuring an accumulation of capital and increased productivity. Management attention increasingly goes to maintenance of structure (connectedness) and sustained resource production. However, the increased complexity and structure generally contributes to an increasing vulnerability to external variations or disturbances. This combination of apparent stability and increased vulnerability results in the ultimate trap of Planet Simple.

Before the onset of resilience science, it was assumed that human-natural systems developed toward a single-equilibrium set of components, relationships, and feedbacks (Nature Balanced). System change was assumed to proceed from loosely organized new entrants (e.g., species, innovators, policy ideas) that take advantage of vacant niches, that are eventually supplanted by mature players whose tight competitive relationships bind resources and preclude entry from competitors. Nature Balanced assumed that if the equilibrium state is disturbed, over time a similar growth-to-production progression would ensure eventual return of the equilibrium state. If Nature Balanced were accurate, system progress could be represented by the front loop alone, as systems were assumed to simply oscillate between growth and production phases as disturbance came and went. Once resilience science unearthed the reality that equilibrium arrangements can fundamentally change after a disturbance (i.e., multiple equilibria), the front loop was deemed an incomplete representation of ecosystem change on its own.[101]

The Ultimate Trap of Planet Simple

A key lesson of resilience science is that, although systems appear stable while in the production phase, this stability is an illusion. On Planet Simple, the production phase is the ultimate endpoint expected to remain stable over time. Given its productivity and apparent stability, managers may aspire to hold human-natural systems in the production phase and drive increased efficiency of outputs. Imposing a static goal on a dynamic system (i.e., trying to hold it in the production phase and optimize resource flow indefinitely), however, leads to the ultimate trap of Planet Simple.

Planet Simple approaches to managing resources (human, capital, raw materials, etc.) that focus on narrowly optimizing for some product, fail to acknowledge the limits to predictability inherent in the ever-changing human-natural systems of Planet Earth. The trap arises because the apparent stability and connectedness of the production phase encourages management to reduce variability and enforce rigidity—both of which result in the system becoming an accident waiting to happen.

Resilience science has shown us that in a complex evolving world, the function and future of linked human-natural systems evolve and are highly uncertain. Efforts to freeze or restore to a static, pristine state, or to establish a fixed condition are inadequate, irrespective of whether the motive is to conserve nature, to exploit a resource for economic gain, to sustain rec-reation, or to facilitate development. Short-term success of narrow efforts to preserve and hold constant can establish a chain of ever more costly surprises—the ultimate trap of Planet Simple.[102]

The adaptive cycle accommodates the reality of tipping points and multiple climax states (also known as multiple equilibria, or multiple stable states) by incorporating the back loop, that is, the phases of *destruction* and *renewal*.[103] Destruction occurs when the tightly bound accumulation of system components, structure, and connections from the production phase is "released" by disturbance such as forest fires, social revolt, or market collapse (we will explore the mechanics of these interactions later in this chapter). The use of destruction borrows from the concept of "creative destruction" whereby the downfall of companies that held a degree of monopoly power allows the entrance of multiple entrepreneurial innovators.[104]

The destruction phase is quickly followed by the renewal phase, where the system is renewed or a new system emerges, leading to the growth phase of a new cycle. The reorganization that occurs during the renewal phase allows novel recombinations to seed experiments that lead to innovations in the next cycle and perhaps catapult the system to a different system state. The components and conditions of the renewal phase, therefore, determine whether an ecosystem will recover following disturbance and continue to provide desired functions or undergo a regime shift and transition to a new, potentially less desirable, state.[105]

The adaptive cycle helps us understand the perils of managing for efficiency and where to focus on innovation, but how can we better understand the interactions between a system (the ball) and its external environment (the basin)? For this, we turn to the concept of panarchy.

Panarchy: The Crown Jewel of Resilience Science

The following question will introduce the most significant contribution of resilience science to our understanding of reality: What do the Arab Spring, a forest fire, and a union strike have in common?

In the Arab Spring, grassroots uprising led to the toppling of government. In a forest fire, the buildup of leaf litter sets the stage for the whole forest to ignite. In a union strike, workers band together to halt an entire industry. In each case, the actions at small scale (e.g., the scale of an individual, leaf, or locality) trigger instability at a higher scale—the government, forest, or industry.

Getting to grips with the concept of *scale* is not easy. It is the concept that I have found most difficult to communicate and the one that is the subject of many unfinished papers. But I keep trying because it is critical for understanding how resilience science explains system change.

Empirical research has established that hierarchical structures emerge in real-world systems—the more complex a system is, the more hierarchical levels are present.[106] These hierarchical levels emerge because of patterns of interactions and feedbacks among system components at different scales of space and time. Understanding these scales is a key aspect of managing complex systems, because management that is not matched to the scale of the problem is limited in its ability to meet its objectives over the long term.[107]

A business is a system that exists at the organizational scale. Businesses emerge from the collective actions of people, who are also systems at the individual scale (and an individual emerges from the collective actions of cells, tissue, and biological feedbacks). Businesses operate within countries that are systems at the national scale. In this way, a business emerges from the collective operation of individual systems nested within it, while at the same time being one system nested among many others that comprise a distinct nation-state (Figure 5).

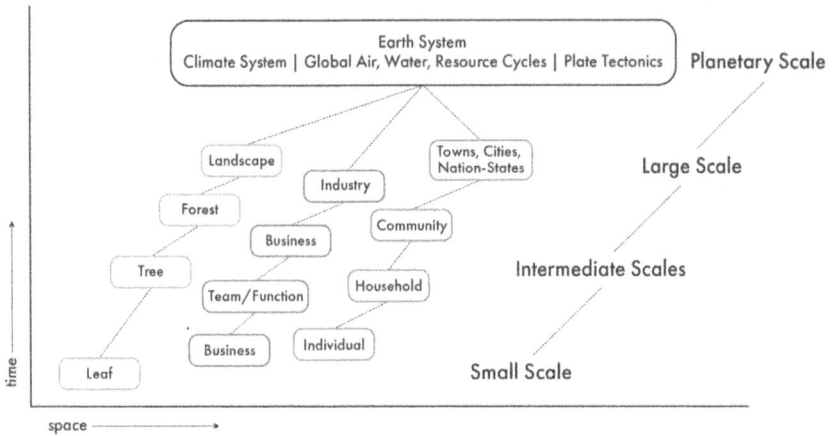

Figure 5. Examples of structure and interactions across different scales of space and time, all of which occur within the planetary scale of Planet Earth.

Resilience scientists found that the resilience of a system state depends strongly on the influences from states and dynamics at scales above and below the focal system.[108] Put another way, a system's trajectory along its adaptive cycle depends on interactions with larger- and smaller-scale systems, each of which is also progressing along its own adaptive cycle. The importance of cross-scale interactions led to the formalization of panarchy theory, which describes the evolving and dynamic nature of adaptive cycles that are nested one within the other across space and time scales.[109]

The word *panarchy* is a scientific portmanteau, coined by combining the word *pan* with the root *archy*. Pan was the Greek god of nature, part animal and part human, who scattered discord, chaos, and ensuing panic. *Archy* is derived from the Latin and Greek words for "rules" and is cognate with words such as *monarchy* ("one ruler") and *hierarchy* ("sacred rules"). Hence, *panarchy* describes the rules of nature or nature's rules.[110]

If panarchy is nature's rules, then panarchy explains how things work on Planet Earth. Systems are not static and equilibrium seeking, they are dynamic and nonstationary. System behavior emerges, often unpredictably, from the collective action of its components—which themselves are systems operating at finer scales. System change is defined by the adaptive cycle and is influenced by interactions with other systems operating at broader and finer scales.

Although resilience science has disproved Planet Simple assumptions of stability and linear change, this does not mean that we are all helpless passengers simply riding the waves of change. By offering a more realistic worldview, resilience and panarchy theory give us the tools we need to understand and manage through change on Planet Earth.

USING PANARCHY TO UNDERSTAND SYSTEM CHANGE

Although the conservation ethos of Teddy Roosevelt is admired by many, the conservation movement has also been guilty of imposing a static goal on dynamic systems. Roosevelt himself summed up the intent when speaking of the Grand Canyon in 1903:

> I want to ask you to keep this great wonder of nature as it now is. I hope you will not have a building of any kind, not a summer cottage, a hotel or anything else to mar the wonderful grandeur, the sublimity, the great loneliness and beauty of the canyon. Leave it as it is.[111]

In many parts of the world, conservationists took hold of large tracts of forests that had been subject to mosaic burning by indigenous populations for millennia and sought to *leave it as it is*. Enforcing stability in the forest enabled the buildup of leaf litter to levels previously unseen, fueling intense, destructive fires leading to significant loss of flora and fauna. Many forest managers now accept the human-in-the-landscape technique of small-scale mosaic burning to support resilience at the scale of the forest.

In the Arab Spring, popular uprisings were able to topple the dictators that had held onto power the longest. The longer the dictators tried to impose their own stability on the system, the more fragile it became as everything changed within and around it. Many democracies recognize this trap and enforce regular elections to ensure the resilience of the nation as a whole.

Popular uprisings and forest fires describe a type of cross-scale interaction labeled as *revolt* in panarchy theory. The other cross-scale interactions are *crisis*, *memory*, and *innovation*. Revisiting the language of the adaptive cycle, a revolt is when the prevalence of *destruction* within systems at lower scale is sufficient to trigger instability and destruction in systems at scales above.

Instability in a system may also arise from change at broader scales, referred to as *crisis* in panarchy theory. Global climate change, loss of social cohesion, and tsunamis are all higher-scale crises that can trigger instability at the scale of a business, household, and local community. A key finding of panarchy theory is that the more rigidity a system has built up over time (in the *production* phase of the adaptive cycle), the more vulnerable it is to *revolt* and *crisis* (Figure 6).

MEMORY

System renewal will depend on the context set by the higher scale (existing laws, cultural norms, ecosystem services)

CRISIS

Higher-scale instability triggers instability in the focal system, by changing the context within which the focal system operates (climate change, political coups)

FOCAL SYSTEM

Production

Renewal

Destruction

Growth

INNOVATION

System destruction opens the door for new actors and ideas to guide renewal. (cultural, political, and biological diversity)

REVOLT

Instability within focal system components (ie at lower scales) cascades up to instability in the focal system (local pollution, social unrest)

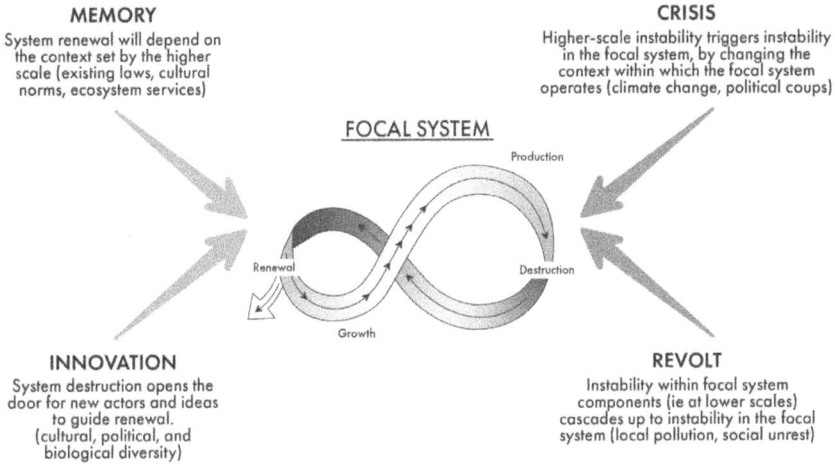

Figure 6. Panarchy theory has enabled us to explain how changes from within a system, as well as from broader scales, can catalyze crisis and renewal within a focal system.

The cross-scale interactions of *memory* and *innovation* influence system renewal after the destruction phase. Following a fire in a forested landscape (perhaps caused by revolt dynamics), the seed bank, physical structures, surviving species, anything arriving from the wider landscape, and the prevailing weather conditions all provide the raw material for the renewal phase.[112] This raw material is the *memory* and includes "the accumulated experience and history of the system, [which] provides context and sources for renewal, recombination, innovation, novelty and self-organization following disturbance."[113]

Recall the suggestion that adaptive opportunity lies within the renewal phase of the adaptive cycle. Panarchy gives further guidance as to how to harness this opportunity by suggesting that during this phase, the maintenance or injection of desired sources of memory from the broader landscape is critical for renewal of desired functions.

Renewal often follows crisis, hence the saying, *never let a good crisis go to waste*—only after a crisis is there the openness to adapt and evolve.

While memory provides the context for renewal, *innovation* provides the raw ingredients. In a Nature Evolving world, novelty and diversity are required in order to allow the system to evolve as the contours of stability basins change. Innovation and diversity, therefore, are critical to ensuring landscapes can adapt and renew in the face of change such that desired functions are maintained. Flowing on from these insights, however, is that in order to manage for resilience, management must be able to *learn* both about changes to the system so they can anticipate the need for changes in management, and about which innovations are worth promoting in order to harness any opportunities change may bring. We will revisit the importance of learning in chapter 6.

The Explanatory Power of Resilience Science

The best part about resilience science is how much it describes life in the real world, Planet Earth, not on some fictitious planet where we think (hope?) we live: Planet Simple.

Let's look at a couple examples from the real world, one from the world of productive ecosystems and one from the world of political systems. In each case, we will see how the phases of the adaptive cycle describe a recurring pattern of rapid, then slowing growth, then swift destruction, and then renewal.[114]

NATURAL ECOSYSTEMS—FISHERIES

Fisheries are excellent examples of human-natural systems that exhibit adaptive cycle dynamics.

Growth Phase: In the absence of human fishing activity, an aquatic or marine ecosystem will have a range of fish and other organisms. Once discovered by humans, a new fishery often sees rapid growth in fishing effort as fishers seek to capitalize on the abundant resources. The initial high returns on investment lure more fishers into the industry.

Production Phase: The fishery reaches a form of human-natural system equilibrium. The number of fish being born roughly matches those being consumed by predators, which now includes humans. This point is commonly referred to as the maximum sustainable yield—the largest catch that can be taken from a fishery's stock over an indefinite period without causing a population decline.

As I mentioned earlier in this chapter, the concept of maximum sustainable yield is an example of the pathology of Planet Simple in action. Optimizing extraction for the maximum sustainable yield leaves no margin for error—successful only if fishing operations do not exceed the quota and if environmental conditions remain stable enough to ensure enough regrowth of stock each year.

Destruction Phase: As fishing pressures intensify, fish populations may decrease below critical thresholds or may become vulnerable to disease because of reduced genetic diversity. Fishing operations remain incentivized to return a stable catch year after year and continue fishing despite the decline in fish populations. Eventually, the fishery collapses. The decline can be swift, the contagion spreading to leave local communities dependent on the fishery economically devastated.

Renewal Phase: The conditions of the renewal phase, including cross-scale interactions of *memory* and *innovation*, will determine whether the fishery recovers to a similar state that occurred prior to the collapse or will never recover.

In the absence of heavy fishing pressure, fish populations may begin to recover. The species makeup may be similar to before the collapse, but *memory* and *innovation* influences such as climate change, pollution, and coral bleaching may result in a different makeup of fish populations better suited to the new conditions. A reevaluation of fishing practices may lead to a revival of the fishery, or government programs to diversify economic activity may cause some to seek alternative livelihoods.

POLITICAL SYSTEMS—ARAB SPRING

The Arab Spring of the early 2010s offers another example of adaptive cycle dynamics and cross-scale interactions.

Rising tensions at the Individual Scale: Several Arab nations experienced increasing societal pressures including high unemployment, especially among the youth; economic disparities; political corruption; lack of political freedoms; and issues of police brutality and repression.

Political Regimes Enforce Stability at the Country Scale: Many of the regimes in the region had been in power for extended periods, maintaining a sense of stability (often surface level) through centralized control, censorship, and suppression of dissent. The established political elite resisted significant reforms, and the societal contract was often based on an understanding of stability in exchange for political passivity. The political regime's resistance to change, despite shifting dynamics at individual and broader scales (most notably the diffusion of information and capacity for collective action enabled by the internet), set the stage for revolt dynamics.

Revolt Dynamics Lead to Destruction: The self-immolation of a Tunisian street vendor, Mohamed Bouazizi, in protest against police corruption acted as a catalyst. Protests in Tunisia led to the ousting of President Ben Ali. This success inspired similar movements across the region, notably in Egypt, Libya, Yemen, Syria, and Bahrain. The long-standing structures of power in some of these countries were quickly (and sometimes violently) dismantled. Panarchy theory suggests that the longer a focal system enforces stability, the more rigidity and vulnerability it accumulates, setting the stage for rapid destruction when overwhelmed by cross-scale dynamics.

Renewal Depends on Memory at the Broader Scale: The availability of institutional memory will influence whether system reorganization will produce a stronger, more productive system or whether it will fall into what resilience scientists call a poverty trap.

Of the countries affected by the Arab Spring, Tunisia is the one that has emerged with a renewed democracy that has remained relatively stable. This result can be explained by the presence of institutional memory that fostered the creation of a functional democracy at the national scale. These aspects of institutional memory include established labor unions, other civil society groups, and relatively progressive social and educational policies established by Tunisia's first president (and that endured through subsequent regimes).

Planet Simple Trap: Engineering Resilience

This Planet Simple trap involves the meaning of resilience itself. Since the introduction of resilience into scientific literature by C. S. Holling over five decades ago, multiple meanings of the concept have appeared.[115] Of note is the distinction made between engineering resilience and evolutionary resilience.[116] Engineering resilience refers to bouncing back after a disruption—the faster the bounce back, the more resilient something is. This definition is linked to the dominance of the Planet Simple mindset, particularly that natural systems gravitate toward a single equilibrium and that system interactions are governed by linear relationships constant over space and time (i.e., Nature Balanced). Resilience scientist Lance Gunderson described how engineering resilience is linked with desires of control and resisting change, saying that engineering resilience relies on "an implicit assumption of global stability. [That is,] there is only one equilibrium or steady state or, if other operating states exist, they should be avoided by applying safeguards."[117] A consequence of engineering resilience is that given the assumption of a single equilibrium, the focus is on staying the same in the face of change rather than allowing system evolution. Managing for engineering resilience "focuses on maintaining efficiency of function, constancy of the system, and a predictable world near a single steady state. It is about resisting disturbance and change, to conserve what you have."[118]

Engineering resilience may be contrasted with evolutionary resilience, which aligns with the Nature Evolving caricature of nature. Managing for evolutionary resilience "is not only about being persistent or robust to disturbance. It is also about the opportunities that disturbance opens up in terms of recombination of evolved structures and processes, renewal of the system and emergence of new trajectories."[119] According to resilience scientist Carl Folke, this "aspect of resilience that concerns the capacity for renewal, reorganization and development...has been less in focus but is essential for the sustainability discourse."[120]

— — — — — — — — — — — — — — — — — — — —

PANARCHY EXPLAINS CONTEMPORARY CLIMATE CHANGE

Earlier in this chapter, I mentioned the importance of philosophy for challenging ideas that may appear obvious but that are fundamentally mistaken. We now realize (often reluctantly) that the unintended consequences of our Planet Simple mindset have become existential threats. The reality of human-induced climate change is hard to believe. Even if we accept that humans exist within the climate system, the idea that humans can *change* the climate system seems absurd.

However, although climate change has inserted a significant danger into our lives, it has also helped usher in a new resilience mindset for Planet Earth (recall the Holderlin quote from the start of Part II—*where there is danger, that which will save us also grows*).[121] Panarchy theory gives us the tools to make the connection between our individual lives and global climate change. While any one person is unlikely to change the climate system in their lifetime, panarchy encourages us to consider changes across scales of space and time. Humans are now a global species, a relatively recent and unprecedented situation at the scale of the Earth. Humans have also contributed to steady increases in greenhouse gases over many lifetimes, now at concentrations also unprecedented in known history.

When our activity is considered at broader scales of space (humans are a global species) and time (human activity accumulated over generations), we can see revolt dynamics at play. Just like the buildup of leaf litter, social angst, and worker dissatisfaction can *scale up* to catalyze wider system change, human activity has *scaled up* to affect the global climate system.

Recalling the assumed equilibrium of microeconomics discussed in chapter 1, it has been observed that "The highest hierarchical scale within microeconomic theory is the economy as a whole, which is believed to automatically maintain a dynamic equilibrium. There is no recognition that the economy itself is sustained and contained by our finite planetary ecosystem."[122] If there ever were a time to revisit our economic worldview, it is now.

The global climate system has enjoyed a period of relative stability over the last ten thousand years, a stability that has been behind significant advances in human civilization. Resilience scientists have noted that "[m]odern humans are drivers in a global regime shift, with high degrees of uncertainty regarding what alternative regime might emerge."[123] Humanity's revolt has thrown the global climate into instability, and panarchy theory suggests that instability at the global scale can cascade down to crisis at national and organizational scales.

The stability of the last ten thousand years has been replaced with a profound uncertainty about what comes next. The implications of this uncertainty for corporate strategy is the subject of the next chapter. Closing this one, I will review and reinforce the fundamentals of how Planet Earth works and what we can do to manage for the real world.

Getting to Planet Earth

Resilience science has shown us that if we want to manage for the reality of Planet Earth, we must revisit our mindset and assume:

- Change instead of Stability

- Connectedness instead of Individuality

- Complexity instead of Measurability

- Discontinuity instead of Predictability

- Nonlinearity instead of Linearity

- Tipping points instead of Equilibrium

	PLANET SIMPLE	PLANET EARTH
How We Think the World Works	Stable	Change
	Individual	Connected
	Measurable	Complex
	Predictable	Discontinuous
	Linear	Nonlinear
	Equilibrium	Tipping points

This mindset shift has profound implications for corporate strategy and decision-making, which remain stuck on Planet Simple. These implications will be discussed in chapters 5 and 6.

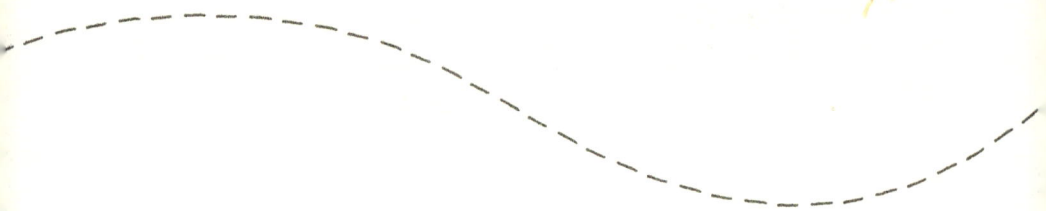

CHAPTER 5

Decision-Making on Planet Earth

Science cannot solve the ultimate mystery of nature. And that is because, in the last analysis, we ourselves are part of nature and therefore part of the mystery that we are trying to solve.

—Max Planck

What is the relationship between knowledge and uncertainty?

Many of us perceive uncertainty as a wilderness. The act of research serves to domesticate and tame the wild. Learning and discovery expand the frontier, diminishing the extent of the unknown. Similarly, you may perceive knowledge as filling a container, progressively plugging holes in our understanding. Uncertainty may present as gaps in an incomplete theory, whereas a complete theory fills the container or covers the terrain.

If we feel that learning and discovery diminish the extent of the unknown, then we imply that research always reduces uncertainty. If we feel that knowledge fills a container, and that a complete theory is possible, we imply that uncertainty is finite and that our knowledge can be complete. Containers may be filled, holes may be plugged, and frontiers may advance to conquer the unknown.

Now consider an alternative. What if the unknown is an ocean, and knowledge is an island? As we increase our knowledge, the size of our island grows. As our island grows, however, the border of our island grows longer and in contact with more of the unknown. In this situation, uncertainty is incapable of elimination. Research can expand our knowledge, but it often uncovers even more uncertainty.[124]

On Planet Simple, assumptions of stability and equilibrium allow us to assume that we can know the laws of nature, that we can predict the future with enough certainty to inform our decisions, and that more research will reduce uncertainty. Having been introduced to the reality of Planet Earth in chapter 4, we now know better.

This chapter takes aim at the decision-making culture of Planet Simple and introduces an alternative better suited for the reality of Planet Earth. It is a thick chapter that goes deep in order to uproot entrenched practice and clear the path for a new mindset. The depth is necessary given this book's ambition to challenge the fundamentals of knowledge that underpin corporate culture. As Girod-Seville and Perret stated in *Doing Management Research: A Comprehensive Guide*, questioning the fundamentals of knowledge "is vital to serious research, as through it researchers can establish the validity and legitimacy of their work."[125]

	PLANET SIMPLE	PLANET EARTH
How We Think the World Works	Stable Individual Measurable Predictable Linear Equilibrium	Change Connected Complex Discontinuous Nonlinear Tipping points
How We Make Decisions	The world is fully knowable Certainty is possible	The world is not fully knowable Uncertainty is always present
Our Business Objectives	Technical rationality Optimization Efficiency	Procedural rationality Robustness Resilience

Planet Simple and Spurious Certitude

In chapter 1, we reviewed how the Planet Simple mindset is fueled by our propensity to see ourselves as separate to nature combined with the reductionist view of progress from the Enlightenment. Isaiah Berlin refers to three propositions of Enlightenment thinking:[126]

- all genuine questions can be answered (and that if a question cannot be answered it is not a question),

- that all these answers are knowable, and

- that all answers must be compatible with one another.

He observes that these propositions came to dominate not just academic philosophy but the business of life itself.[127]

Since the Enlightenment, our view of the world has been single, knowable, consistent, certain, fixed, and finite. It has been a world we can master—a world that we *should* master in order to achieve Bacon's ideal society (as described in chapter 1). Psychiatrist Iain McGilchrist noted how this mindset "was inevitably a simulacrum substituted for the ever-changing and evolving, never graspable actuality of experience, [but] was nonetheless taken for a reality."[128] To follow McGil-christ's logic, we may say that corporate sustainability is about shifting the mindset of business from Planet Simple to the ever-changing and evolving, never graspable reality of Planet Earth, described better by resilience science.

An investigation on the relationship between the human mind and the external world is beyond the scope of this book. At the same time, this chapter is about how people make decisions. If the Planet Simple mind presumes that certainty is possible (or at least is preferable to acknowledging uncertainty), the information it receives about the external world will be made to cohere with the Planet Simple mindset, and so will any decision that flows from it. Even when presented with information to the contrary, our view of the world as single, knowable, consistent, certain, fixed, and finite *is nonetheless taken for a reality*. Revising the structure of scientific revolutions described by Kuhn, information about the real world will be made to conform with the box supplied by the existing paradigm—Planet Simple.

Hinting at the linkage between sustainability and mindset, sus-tainability challenges have been described as "wicked" problems. Wicked problems may be contrasted with "tame" problems, where an exhaustive formulation can be stated containing all the information the problem-solver needs for understanding and solving the problem. Wicked problems, on the other hand, resist exhaustive formulation. Understanding of the problem will always be incomplete, and some uncertainties will not be reducible as time goes on. This means that wicked problems will be defined with partial, incomplete understand-ing, and this partial understanding will frame the proposed solutions, which will also be incomplete. For wicked problems, therefore, there are no true or false answers. Rather, solutions may be "good or bad," "better or worse," or simply "good enough."[129]

In the previous chapter, we described the worldview of resilience science, a worldview that has been shown to "quite simply describe reality better" than Planet Simple. Since Holling's seminal work over fifty years ago, resilience scientists have found the adaptive cycle and panarchy to be the easy work. It has been far more difficult to translate resilience science into organizational policy, strategy, and practice.

One of Holling's students, now Professor Lance Gunderson at Emory University, ran into a persistent challenge when trying to implement resilience science as a botanist in the US National Park Service. He found that managers seemed more interested in seeking *spurious certitude* by focusing on what is "known," even if the problems were wicked by nature and the resulting management recommendations were irrelevant or even pathological.[130] This chapter will show how spurious certitude happens when we try to force the reality of Planet Earth into the "inflexible box" of the Planet Simple mindset.

Planet Simple and Technical Rationality

On Planet Simple, equilibrium dynamics and linear assumptions give rise to an apparent stability that seems predictable over time. Because Planet Simple is knowable and finite, any research effort is assumed to advance the frontiers of our knowledge, progressively plugging data gaps on the way to a complete theory of the laws of nature governing our world. More research will lead to better data, which leads to more complete models, and ultimately to better decisions.

The table at the beginning of this chapter included *technical rationality* as a component of the Planet Simple mindset. Technical rationality is a mode of decision-making based on the Planet Simple metaphor of linear progress, absolute truth, and rational planning.[131] It is characterized by centralized decision-making and linear, step-by-step implementation. Decisions rely on extensive research to reduce uncertainty and employ formal methods and metrics to evaluate alternatives (matrices, multi-criteria decision analyses, Monte Carlo simulations, and so on). Research and impersonal methods are prerequisites for rational decisions, where the objective is to find the optimal way to achieve targets as efficiently as possible.

Technically rational decision-making has visions of predictability and control over issues to which it is applied, guided by the assumption that science can arrive at "discrete, comprehensive policy" featuring "the one best way" to solve the issue.[132] Guided by technical rationality, Planet Simple thinks science and technology can tame even the most wicked of problems.

Technical rationality relies on science to be objective, comprehensive, and provide enough certainty as to everything important to decision-makers. The expectation of a linear relationship between research, knowledge, and decision-making is "predicated upon the presumptions that science can predict with certainty and clarity what will happen in the physical world, and decision-making is a [technically] rational process. None of these is true."[133]

While many have called the assumptions of linear, technically rational decision-making into question, it is still the case that many executives, investors, scientists, and members of the lay public believe that such a linear process does or should occur.[134] As suggested by Ascher and colleagues:

> Major segments of the aware public and some policymakers
> embrace the notion that scientific 'findings,' once confirmed
> to the satisfaction of reputable scientists, can be taken as valid.
> Analysis and decisions can flow directly from these established
> findings. This notion ignores, of course, the omnipresence of
> uncertainty and neglects the questioning of the normative

bases that have already gone into the generation, screening, and analysis of the knowledge.[135]

Keep in mind that my argument is not anti-science. I am addressing the expectations placed on science—an enterprise whose existence depends on acknowledging uncertainty—to achieve *certainty* as the foundation of *rational* decision-making.

TECHNICAL RATIONALITY IN THE REAL WORLD

Buoyed by the Planet Simple mindset, the emergence of an environmental challenge such as climate change or nature loss stimulates an almost automatic call for scientific prediction as the first step toward meeting the challenge.[136] In turn, climate prediction and projections have become "without a doubt the bedrock" of climate-related decision-making.[137]

To meet this perceived need, a "prediction enterprise" featuring public and private research programs focused heavily on developing predictive modeling capacity has emerged.[138] Evidence of the prediction enterprise is seen in initiatives of the Intergovernmental Panel on Climate Change (IPCC), as well as other programs such as the International Geosphere-Biosphere Programme (IGBP) and the US Global Change Research Program, which have at their core the desire to predict global change under the assumption that such research must be the basis for recommended policy actions.[139]

There are consequences in assuming that predictive models of the total Earth climate are *required* foundations for *rational* decision-making. At the most fundamental level, because climate models are based on data that is *known*, they have to have a degree of fixity and continuity—if the discontinuous and constantly changing nature of the Earth system is respected, it cannot be *known*.[140] Technically rational decision-making on Planet Simple cannot tolerate uncertainty, however, so climate models need to tweak reality to fit the demands of decision-makers. Again, we find ourselves on Planet Simple trying to fit reality into our existing box.

Some of the ways reality is distorted to fit the models include:

- *Measurability Over Importance:* The omission of factors based on measurability rather than importance results in failed model projections that are attributed to events such as unusual storms, floods, winds, or other unanticipated occurrences. The real-life surprises that result in inaccurate projections are often caused by an omitted process, which was incorrectly assumed to be unimportant.[141] The reality is that Earth system complexity requires modelers to make assumptions as to which factors to include, exclude, and emphasize. This reality introduces subjective considerations into what are perceived to be comprehensive and essential foundations for rational decision-making and allows for the dangerous assumption that what is excluded is also unimportant.

- *Illusion of Completeness:* Because completeness in knowledge is impossible on Planet Earth, researchers must be selective in what they include in a model and make assumptions to account for uncertainties. This means that only a fraction of the various parameters, relationships, and events that constitute natural systems may be expressed in equations that comprise a predictive model.[142] But because What We See Is All There Is (recall Kahneman's WYSIATI from chapter 1), we rarely acknowledge that climate models are incomplete. We end up blinded by surprises that were omitted for convenience rather than importance.

- *Difficulty with High-Impact, Low-Probability Events:* Technical limitations of predictive models result in inadequate incorporation of negative impacts of unknown or low-probability events.[143] Given the disproportionately high contribution such events have in shaping human-natural systems, the inability to predict them "implies the inability to predict history."[144]

The difficulty with high-impact, low-probability events is notable given the ultimate objective of climate-related risk management is to reduce the impact of climate change and promote adaptation. This was revealed in harsh reality during 2023's devastating Hurricane Otis at Mexico's southern coast near Acapulco. Otis intensified from a tropical storm to Category 5 in less than twenty-four hours and pummeled the coast with an intensity that no one expected. Climate models had suggested a range of intensification trajectories, per the solid lines in Figure 7. The dotted line is the actual. What a shame the false sense of security the models must have provided to everyone on the ground!

Examples like this show how climate projections should be one, but not the only, mechanism used to inform climate adaptation—particularly given the reality that they are so bad at projecting extremes, and it is the extremes that reshape lives and landscapes. People don't die from mean temperatures; they die from the extremes.

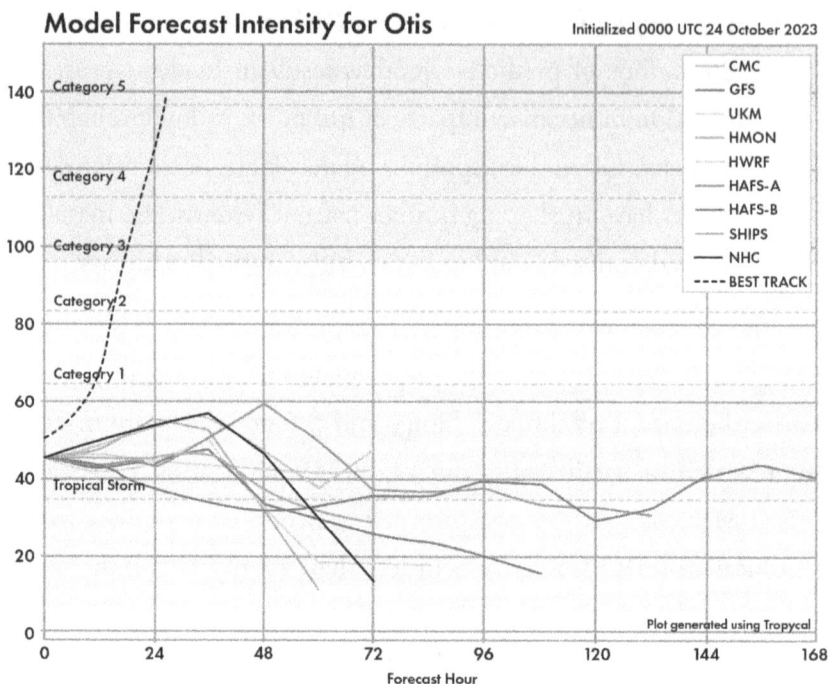

Jeff Burgess, Twitter post, April 24, 2023, 7:38 p.m.,
https://twitter.com/burgwx/status/1717012912999391235.

Figure 7. Intensity forecasts from a variety of models used routinely to predict
hurricane behavior. The official National Hurricane Center forecast is shown in black.
All of these forecasts were produced on Monday night, October 23, about thirty-one
hours before Otis made landfall.

SPURIOUS CERTITUDE AND PRETENDED KNOWLEDGE

Predictive models remain unable to comprehend influential yet low-probability extreme events and hard-to-measure social phenomena, among other factors. By focusing on what is known at the expense of the unknown, predictive methods often result in overconfidence in the accuracy and completeness of the pictures they produce.[145] They appear to tame problems that, in fact, remain wicked.

On Planet Simple, however, rather than making uncertainties transparent, researchers and decision-makers alike obfuscate, ignore, or exclude uncertainties associated with projections in their research or models. Failing to acknowledge uncertainties underlying our understanding of complex systems results in a mismatch between the sense of certainty in the projection and the real level of uncertainty facing decision-makers.[146]

The apparent rigor associated with technical, quantitative approaches results in decision-makers and the lay public incapable of challenging the projections. This also leads to a bias where modeled projections are thought to be less uncertain, and thus preferred within a Planet Simple mindset that demands certainty over alternative, qualitative strategies incorrectly presumed to be less objective. The technical proficiency of projections conveys the impression that the analysis is not only rigorous but also complete, despite the fact that climate models are always *incomplete* (as discussed on the previous pages).[147]

Credibility-seeking behavior by modelers, many of whom sell the data to businesses desperate for *the one best answer*, can also result in a failure to communicate underlying uncertainties. Ascher and colleagues define credibility seeking as "the tendency for scientists and lay people to generate, transmit, or use knowledge that appears to be more rigorous or valid than other types of knowledge, which often leads to the neglect of other valuable knowledge."[148] Furthermore, "experts often suppress information or insights that they regard as less rigorous and therefore less scientifically defensible in order both to maintain what they view as the integrity of their disciplines and to protect their personal reputations."[149] By the time decision-makers get the "knowledge...it is often shorn of its caveats or any explicit statements of its questionable assumptions."[150] Furthermore, researchers Pilkey and Pilkey-Jarvis have found it common for "virtually devastating problems and uncertainties" to exist within model projections, "but in the end the model is recommended for use."[151]

Even if modelers were completely transparent about uncertainties and caveats, decision-makers on Planet Simple ignore expressions of uncertainty because of the need to be decisive when decisiveness is seen as a virtue.[152] Decision-makers are thus the "clients" within a Planet Simple decision-making framework that expects certainty in planning, even if it is spurious. This human attraction to certainty clashes directly with the reality of wicked problems that underlie corporate sustainability. These problems offer vast, irreducible uncertainties combined with a sense of urgency from investors, customers, executives, and the lay public. Nobel laureate Daniel Kahneman wrote on similar challenges in medicine, a pursuit also marked by wicked problems, extreme uncertainty, and urgency:

> Experts who acknowledge the full extent of their ignorance may expect to be replaced by more confident competitors, who are better able to gain the trust of clients. An unbiased appreciation of uncertainty is a cornerstone of rationality— but it is not what people and organizations want. Extreme uncertainty is paralyzing under dangerous circumstances, and the admission that one is merely guessing is especially unacceptable when the stakes are high. Acting on pretended knowledge is often the preferred solution.[153]

Over thirty years ago, Professor John Robinson of the University of Toronto observed that "the basing of policy on supposedly neutral forecasts allows decision-making institutions to assume a cloak of objectivity."[154] Like the "pretended knowledge" described by Kahneman, the technical rationality of Planet Simple favors the comfortable yet spurious certitude of climate models, and the presumed objectivity and rigor with which they are based, rather than acknowledging the full extent of uncertainty.

I should pause here to remind the reader that my argument relates to the application of predictive models within a Planet Simple mindset that assumes certainty and completeness in knowledge. I recognize that climate models are based on rigorous research built up over generations by dedicated people, but these people will confess to you that their understanding remains incomplete. However, in a world presumed to be knowable, incomplete understanding is seen as a deficiency instead of as reality.

Planet Simple Trap: Outcome Vulnerability

This Planet Simple trap distorts the reality of Planet Earth by assuming a linear connection between climate models and corporate decision-making.

I'll start the description of this Planet Simple trap with a story from recent work as part of the BWD Strategic team. Early in one of our engagements, we were discussing climate change with the company's management. The managers presented the outcomes of a climate scenario analysis that they had completed the previous year with the help of another advisory firm. The analysis offered substantial amounts of data on potential future changes across the hundreds of company sites worldwide. Despite the illusion of certainty provided by the extensive quantification and apparent precision of the predictive modeling, there were very real problems regarding how the information could be used to inform decision-making on Planet Earth.

Management recognized that there were few actionable insights among the countless numbers, so they took an alternative approach. They ended up prioritizing sites for climate action based on their importance to the business in terms of revenue generation. Probably without realizing it, the managers fell back on a tried-and-tested approach to climate adaptation called contextual vulnerability assessment. While this was encouraging, I couldn't help but think that they didn't need to spend several hundred thousand dollars on a scenario analysis just to tell them to focus on the sites that generate the most revenue.

In this situation, the trap is Planet Simple's assumption of a linear relationship between research and decision-making—that projections will automatically reveal the way forward for management. Taking this approach to climate change adaptation is referred to as *outcome vulnerability*. Going back to my example, management found outcome vulnerability to be wanting and invoked *contextual vulnerability* to understand the way forward.

What is contextual vulnerability and how does it make up for the shortcomings of Planet Simple?

The technical rationality underpinning Planet Simple decision-making seeks to minimize the influence of contextual factors and achieve the one best answer that can be universally true. Human behavior is deprioritized on Planet Simple because its contextual nature resists the measurability and generalizability required for technical rationality. Criticisms of predictive approaches to climate change adaptation (outcome vulnerability) are well-founded and relate to difficulties accounting for local contextual factors that may interact with any climate changes to affect vulnerability on the ground. Underlying these criticisms is a criticism of technical rationality's reliance on climate models as foundations for rational decision-making and preference for extensive research of national or international scope.

Predictive models generally provide projections at the global or continental scales and omit factors that are difficult to model in the hope they are not important. The reliance on projections when assessing outcome vulnerability thus results in findings that may not account for finer-scale climatic nuances nor have regard to important contextual factors. A focus on modeled climate stressors to the exclusion of contextual factors, therefore, may be insufficient for understanding the impacts on and responses for the organization seeking to adapt.[155]

To overcome the shortcomings of a technically rational approach to planning for climate change adaptation, there have been calls to test and trial alternatives that account for contextual variation and that may provide for more robust planning in the face of uncertainty.[156] *Contextual vulnerability* assessments take a bottom-up approach, considering vulnerability as an asset's, population's, or other system's present inability to cope with changing climatic conditions.

Contextual analysis also helps deal with uncertainty. The focus is on contextual adaptations that can be made now, and that "strengthen the ability to respond to stressors...under present conditions, which should then increase the capacity to respond to changing conditions in the future."[157] By focusing on improving *present* adaptive capacity, adaptation actions resulting from contextual vulnerability assessments focus on enhancing the capacity to adapt to *any* change as opposed to improving adaptive capacity with regard to specific projected future changes. It is for this reason that contextual vulnerability approaches allow for adaptation to uncertainty regarding future change.[158]

Contextual vulnerability also makes use of *temporal analogues*. The point here is that a focus on defining vulnerability primarily through future exposure to climate hazards neglects learning about where vulnerabilities may already exist. Whenever I do a scenario analysis, I always ask for insights on locations/facilities that have already had challenges with climate-related events. If part of the business is already having problems, it is very likely to keep having problems as the situation gets worse.

Despite enjoying some popularity in the 1980s, analogue methodologies have been underutilized in climate change adaptation research ever since—despite being recognized as an important method by the IPCC. Instead, research has "focused predominantly on [outcome] vulnerability assessments. The future, not the past, was the focus of these studies, which aimed to identify future climate impacts on human systems directly attributable to [greenhouse gases] and based on the output of [global circulation models]."[159] IPCC technical guidelines refer to analogue methodologies as useful when assessing contextual vulnerability in particular because they focus on interactions of climate and society in a region—a nod to the interconnectedness of Planet Earth.[160] Furthermore, where outcome vulnerability assessments fail to take the next step and examine opportunities for adaptation, analogues provide for ready identification of potential adaptation actions and may expand on previously restricted options.

Temporal analogues also offer a direct route to the holy grail of corporate climate research according to investors and frameworks like the TCFD and ISSB (introduced in chapter 2)—which is the integration of climate change into corporate strategy and risk management. Leading researchers refer to *mainstreaming* climate change adaptation by identifying existing challenges that may intersect with climate change to exacerbate vulnerability.[161]

Mainstreaming climate change consideration sits in opposition to compiling a standalone adaptation plan that sits separate from existing operations. It helps bridge the gap between knowledge and decision-making that Planet Simple cannot and brings "immediate benefits in the form of reduced sensitivity to climatic risks and increased adaptability."[162]

Planet Earth and Procedural Rationality

Because the foundation of Enlightenment thinking, and by extension the Planet Simple mindset, is that all truths cohere, are mutually compatible, non-contradictory, and ultimately reconcilable, its weak point is where incompatibilities are found. Aristotle's observations of Earth as a round sphere was incompatible to traditional view of the world as flat. Copernicus's observations were incompatible with the view of the Earth at the center of the universe. When these incompatibilities are brought into focus, "we are, and always have been, liberated into another way of looking at the world."[163]

Recalling our metaphors on knowledge and uncertainty from earlier in this chapter, it would seem that the ocean metaphor is a better way of looking at knowledge and decision-making on Planet Earth. Because wicked problems resist exhaustive formulation, efforts to reduce uncertainty reveal previously unrecognized complexities, which in turn increases the uncertainty presented to decision-makers trying to understand the issue. We may increase the size of our island of knowledge, but in doing so, we have increased the size of the boundary between ourselves and the unknown.

The technical rationality of Planet Simple holds that decision-makers can rely on technical research to achieve certainty and completeness of understanding, which would determine the optimal answer for a problem. In *The Sciences of the Artificial*, Dr. Herbert Simon proposed that once realistic assumptions regarding uncertainty and knowledge are taken into account, the problem shifts from finding the *optimal* solution "to finding a way of calculating, very approximately, where a good course of action lies."[164]

Decision-making that acknowledges the reality of Planet Earth relies on *procedural rationality*, instead of technical rationality. Procedural rationality recognizes the reality of uncertainty by shifting the focus from *right* to *good*, from *optimal* to *robust*, from *efficiency* to *resilience*. Because technical rationality assumes certainty prior to a decision, the success of a decision is judged by whether the *outcome* matched the prediction. Procedural rationality judges a decision on the basis of whether the *process* was appropriate for the level of uncertainty facing the decision-maker. This shift toward judging decisions, and by extension business performance, based on *process* instead of *outcome* will be revisited in chapter 9.

Scenario Analysis for Decision-Making

In *The Master and His Emissary*, McGilchrist laments how the analytical and reductionist view of the world offered to us by the left hemisphere of our brain—our emissary—has superseded the holistic view of the world offered to us by our right hemisphere—our master. This is not to say that the analytical and reductionist worldview is worthless, however. In his words:

> I do not underestimate the importance of the left hemisphere's contribution to all that humankind has achieved, and to all

that we are, in the everyday sense of the word; in fact it is because I value it; that I say it has to find its proper place, so as to fulfill its critically important role. It is a wonderful servant, but a very poor master.[165]

I would make the same conclusion regarding our use of modeled projections to inform corporate sustainability.

On Planet Simple, better projections are assumed to do more than reduce the uncertainty in our understanding of how the world works. They are also assumed to reveal the correct prescription that can be fed into decision-making and implemented to resolve the challenge. These assumptions match the linear worldview of Planet Simple, where scientific research and technical models can be taken as complete and that decisions will flow directly from the knowledge.[166]

Addressing the US House of Representatives Science Committee meeting on *New Directions for Climate Research and Technology Initiatives*, Dr. Radford Byerly of the University of Colorado called the linear relationship of research and decision-making into question. He noted that for Planet Earth issues like climate change, "a prediction will not tell us what to do in terms of mitigation and adaptation."[167] Rather, the question of *what to do* involves politics and policy, areas in which climate scientists have little expertise.[168] He was echoing points made just a year or so earlier by Harvard academic David Cash, who wrote that no decision-maker "can be expected to make decisions based on globally averaged values. Their decisions will be largely influenced by local political context, local preferences and constraints, short-term economic needs, the set of options they have available, and their associated local costs and benefits."[169]

When it comes to actually making a decision about what to do, a projection will inform effective decision-making only if it is helpful in discriminating among alternative courses of action in terms of their expected outcomes. The issue for climate change adaptation, however, is that the outcomes of alternative adaptation strategies often depend little on discriminating among various climate predictions.[170]

On Planet Earth, we need to avoid spurious certitude and take a procedurally rational approach to corporate strategy and decision-making. To quote Dr. Simon again, this time from *Reason in Human Affairs*, a characteristic required for procedurally rational decision-making in the face of complexity and uncertainty is "a mechanism for generating alternatives. A large part of our problem solving consists in the search for good alternatives, or for improvements in alternatives we already know."[171]

One such mechanism is scenario analysis. Although scenario analysis had been used in niche circles for decades, its widespread arrival on corporate agenda is relatively recent. In the mid-2010s, the Financial Stability Board (FSB) grew concerned that climate change was not on the radar of corporate boards and executive teams. Year after year, insurers were underestimating the financial losses associated with climate-related events. The world had just signed the Paris Agreement, which all but committed the planet to stop extracting and burning fossil fuels in the coming decades—a policy risk that was not being considered by organizations dependent on energy (which is every company everywhere). Failure to acknowledge, manage, and disclose performance on these climate-related issues threatened the stability of financial markets worldwide. In response, the FSB created the TCFD, which we covered briefly in chapter 2.

An interested reader can find plenty of specifics about the TCFD on its website, or on the website of the International Financial Reporting Standards (IFRS) Foundation (which assumed responsibility for the functions of the TCFD in 2023). The point about the TCFD that I would like to make here is that it represented one of the first mainstream calls for business to move beyond a Planet Simple mindset. The TCFD recognized that business wasn't thinking about climate because it never had to before—after all, the climate system had been stable for at least ten thousand years. It also recognized climate change is taking us into uncharted territory, that humans tend to think the future will be the same as the recent past, and that humans underestimate the impact of low-probability future events (recall the chapter 1 discussion of the comfort of certainty).

To help business leave Planet Simple, the TCFD recommended the use of scenario analysis. Scenario analysis would combat the tendency to plan for short-term time horizons and to assume that the future would be the same as the recent past—both of which are Planet Simple constructs that allow business to assume certainty in their strategic planning. While the use of scenario analysis would be new for many (some businesses had engaged in scenario analysis for decades), the real shock of TCFD was that every company was asked to consider scenario analysis *in relation to climate change*, considered by Planet Simple to be a trivial CSR matter unrelated to core business.

Several characteristics of scenario analysis help business adopt procedural rationality and thus move closer to managing for the reality of Planet Earth. Our discussion here relates to scenario analysis as the appropriate framework for Planet Earth; practical guidance on how to perform a scenario analysis is provided in chapter 8.

SCENARIO ANALYSIS FOCUSES ON PLAUSIBILITY OVER LIKELIHOOD

A scenario is a plausible description about a possible future. Scenarios are based on the idea that futures are not unique and that uncertainties both in drivers and in systems dynamics are so numerous that futures cannot be predetermined. The aim when studying futures with scenarios is to explore possibilities in systems with important uncertainties rather than to predict specific outcomes. The range of possibilities is diverse, as illustrated by the consideration of several scenarios in each scenario analysis.

Focusing on multiple plausible scenarios guards against focusing on probable or likely events to the detriment of including less probable and more uncertain surprises that may have large consequences. Consequence, rather than likelihood, is the metric by which scenarios are compared.[172]

The rise of resilience science has shown us that although it is uncommon for a system to cross a tipping point, it is highly consequential when it happens. Scenarios have been used as part of resilience assessments to explore how future change may result in regime shifts in human-natural systems crossing tipping points with potentially irreversible consequences.[173]

SCENARIO ANALYSIS SEEKS A GOOD OPTION, BECAUSE THERE IS NO BEST OPTION

Scenario analysis lays the groundwork for identifying a range of potential management strategies, thus granting decision-makers a range of alternatives that may be employed in different contexts. In addition to identifying alternatives, scenarios may also be used to assess the alternatives as to their likelihood of success given the range of future uncertainties. A goal of scenario planning is to "identify weak policies and those that are more robust to uncertainty about the future."[174] The school of robust decision-making seeks strategies that perform well compared to alternatives across a wide range of assumptions about the future.[175] With regard to climate change adaptation, established experts have suggested:

Decision-makers systematically examine the performance of their adaptation strategies/policies/activities over a wide range of plausible futures driven by uncertainty about the future state of climate and many other economic, political, and cultural factors. They should choose a strategy that they find sufficiently robust across these alternative futures. Such an approach can identify successful adaptation strategies without accurate and precise predictions of future climate.[176]

Robust decision-making may be contrasted with the optimization-focused decision-making of Planet Simple, which requires certainty in projections in order to settle on the optimal way forward. While a robust strategy may not be optimal for any given scenario, by performing well across a range of futures, a robust strategy equips a business for success against future uncertainties.

SCENARIO ANALYSIS EXPLORES UNCERTAINTY RATHER THAN REDUCING IT

Management on Planet Simple focuses on efficiency and ignores uncertainty in favor of spurious certitude, leading to crisis and reactive management. In contrast, a successful scenario analysis effort should enhance the ability of people to cope with and take advantage of future change.[177] Because scenarios focus on uncertainties and their consequences, they have enabled managers to not only respond to changes but to anticipate them. An important outcome of any scenario analysis process is the identification of factors crucial for success but that are also deeply uncertain. Identifying these uncertainties lays the groundwork for genuine adaptive management in support of organizational learning and resilience (as will be detailed in chapter 6).

━ ━ ━ ━ ━ ━ ━ ━ ━ ━ ━ ━ ━ ━ ━ ━ ━ ━ ━

Planet Simple Trap: Scenario Analysis or Sensitivity Analysis?

This Planet Simple trap distorts scenario analysis by mistaking it for sensitivity analysis, a practice that retains objectives of optimization and control.

On Planet Simple, business optimizes for a target outcome and manages for efficiency. Objectives of optimization and efficiency rely on the underlying Planet Simple assumptions of stability and equilibrium (chapter 1). Pivoting from efficiency to resilience means using scenario analysis to acknowledge uncertainty and achieve robustness across a range of futures (rather than targeting optimization for a "most likely" future). As stated by the Bank of International Settlements: "Scenario analysis is a tool that challenges assumptions. A key feature of the scenarios is to explore alternatives that may significantly after the basis for business-as-usual assumptions. Accordingly, they need to consider extreme but plausible scenarios."[178]

Since the TCFD made scenario analysis an expectation of today's corporations, many so-called scenario analyses have been published that fail to show the underlying mindset shift that resilience requires. To explain, it is important to distinguish between *scenario analysis* and *sensitivity analysis*.[179] Scenario analysis (as described earlier in this chapter) is different to sensitivity analysis where a business tests the capacity of its existing strategy to withstand a challenge (such as a carbon price). Many companies have published climate scenario analyses that are, upon closer inspection, actually sensitivity analyses. It is a nuanced but important distinction for business resilience. Sensitivity analysis imputes the objectives of control and short-term efficiency, with roots in Planet Simple thinking. It does

not support long-term resilience in the same way that scenario
analysis does (Figure 8).

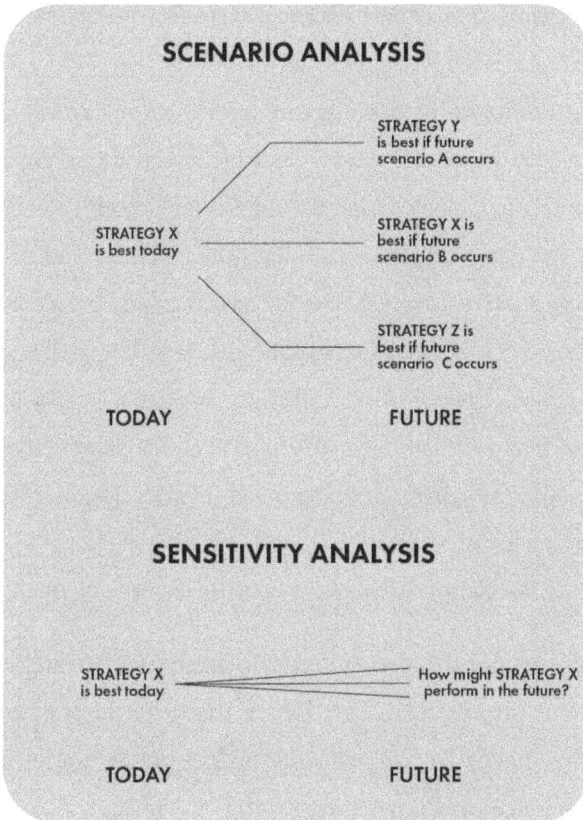

*Figure 8. Scenario analysis asks how a company may need to evolve its strategy
to remain competitive across various future scenarios. Sensitivity analysis does
not openly contemplate other strategies. Instead, it seeks to understand how
future conditions may affect the performance of a particular strategy.*

The sensitivity analyses masquerading as scenario analyses
that I'm thinking of claim to define a percent of financial impact
attributable to climate-related effects, or even to climate change
as a whole. The company may disclose that they are "resilient" to
climate change because the estimated financial effects are less than

2 percent of today's revenue (for example).

Reaching back to the resilience science described in chapter 4, scenario analysis is meant to acknowledge that climate change is a form of instability that affects the entire environment within which a business operates. The business must acknowledge that it is a system within a broader climate system. The intent of scenario analysis is to consider the various ways that the broader climate system may evolve and design a corporate strategy that can succeed across these futures. Sensitivity analysis, by contrast, takes corporate strategy as a given and seeks to minimize the influence of particular risks. Applying climate-related sensitivity analysis in the place of true scenario analysis is fundamentally misplaced, as the effects of the broader climate system, including our policies to mitigate climate impact, cannot be reduced to a single measure of risk.

━ ━ ━ ━ ━ ━ ━ ━ ━ ━ ━ ━ ━ ━ ━ ━ ━ ━ ━

We will revisit the use of scenario analysis in strategic planning and the focus on *process* in Part III. In the next chapter, we will shift toward what needs to happen *after* a decision is made, in order to achieve resilience on Planet Earth.

CHAPTER 6

Adaptive Governance for Planet Earth

> *Understanding how to act under conditions of incomplete information is the highest and most urgent human pursuit.*
>
> —Nassim Nicholas Taleb, *The Black Swan*

The relationship between information and decisions can be split into two parts: information obtained before a decision is made (the *front end* of a decision), and information obtained after a decision is made (the *back end* of a decision). On Planet Simple, decision-making is dominated by the front end. As explained in the previous chapter, the technical rationality of Planet Simple seeks certainty prior to making a decision, even if it takes the form of spurious certitude. This approach results in a disproportionate focus on research and analysis at the front end of a decision because of the widespread belief that if we get the information right, the right decision will flow from it.[180] Time and time again, however, we are surprised by uncertainty. But on Planet Simple, our continued failure to predict the future is taken as a need to double down on our efforts to know the laws of nature, rather than being taken as evidence that our efforts may be fundamentally misplaced.

Instead, if we accept that a complete understanding of the laws of nature is impossible, we recognize that uncertainty will never be eliminated when it comes to managing our business on Planet Earth. The wicked problems described in chapter 5 will never be tamed to the extent that they can be formulated with certainty and addressed with comprehensive and neat solutions. Instead, reducing uncertainty may be achieved through learning from decisions and actions rather than through top-down research and model-building alone. This is the goal of *adaptive management*: to reject the assumption of certainty in decisions and take action in the face of uncertainty with the goal of learning from the action rather than solely from external research. *Adaptive governance*, as I will explain, is the context that allows adaptive management to operate as intended.[181]

Adaptive management focuses on the back end of decision-making—evaluating, reporting, and learning from the results of decisions. Unfortunately, the back end is often ignored or belittled by many business leaders, seen as a burden, or simply another regulatory compliance activity. This needs to change. Monitoring, evaluation, and reporting is vital to resilience because it is the pathway to creating a real learning organization that consistently adapts and outperforms its competitors.

Organizational learning goes hand-in-hand with organizational resilience. While Planet Simple distorts resilience to focus on staying the same, another aspect of resilience crucial for sustainability concerns the capacity for renewal, reorganization, and development in the face of change (see the Planet Simple trap of engineering resilience described in chapter 4).[182] The ability to learn has been linked to adaptive capacity, making it a crucial ingredient for corporate sustainability. A business's ability to learn from its actions will determine whether it successfully anticipates system change or succumbs to spurious certitude and fails to adapt.

Adaptive Management Is True Scientific Management

The Planet Simple mindset is perceived as scientific because it borrows from *The Principles of Scientific Management* defined by Frederick Winslow Taylor (as introduced in chapter 1). However, Taylor's view of science was the partial, reductionist view that has been shown to be inadequate for understanding the reality of Planet Earth.

Assuming certainty in decisions and not evaluating the results is not what any scientist does, yet it is what we do on Planet Simple every day. Business leaders on Planet Simple may think they are practicing scientific management, but Planet Simple decision-making is anything but scientific. Genuine science involves taking action—an experiment—to test a hypothesis and evaluating the results of the action against the hypothesis. It is not a burden for scientists to evaluate the results of their actions (experiments), whereas for many corporate executives, it is a burden to evaluate and disclose the outcomes of their actions. Acknowledging the real level of uncertainty facing a decision-maker means admitting that corporate strategy is an experiment and setting up the procedures to learn from it.

As we discussed in chapter 4, human-natural systems on Planet Earth often gravitate to multiple equilibria, and these systems and their equilibria are likely to change over time (i.e., Nature Evolving).

Building resilience thus requires management that is oriented toward learning about system change because of the inevitable uncertainty facing decision-makers as to present system condition and its trajectory.

Given the complexity and uncertainty related to human-natural systems, it has been argued that they "can never be managed."[183] Rather, "they can only be perturbed and the outcome observed," and "many of these outcomes will likely be unpredictable."[184] Adaptive management rejects the idea that scientific uncertainty must be resolved before actions should be taken because no amount of data or theory will be able to eliminate all uncertainty. Adaptive management presumes wicked problems cannot be tamed, so when it comes to uncertainties facing management, managers "have no choice other than to try to learn from each management decision through a process of evaluation of the results."[185] Because adaptive management realizes strategies are actually questions "masquerading as answers,"[186] a key suggestion of adaptive management is that strategies are experiments: *learn from them.*[187]

Adaptive Management and Loop Learning

Adaptive management has emerged as the only widely recognized model for managing uncertainty and complexity in interactive human-natural systems because its emphasis on evaluation and reporting is the very process through which decision-makers acquire the information necessary to learn.[188] This is a fundamental shift from the technical rationality of Planet Simple, which held that the *only* information that could inform *rational* decisions is external scientific research. Adaptive management "elevates the role of monitoring and evaluation beyond the cosmetic and superficial attention often given these activities to a level at which they become the mechanisms through which significant changes in policy and practice in light of outcomes can occur."[189] Comprehensive appraisal is essential because we learn about the behavior of real-world systems by observation.[190] Moreover, it plays a vital role of generating critical feedback "about the accuracy of our opinions and doubts."[191]

As with several terms in this book, we need to dive a bit deeper into what we mean by *learning*. To do so, we will invoke the concept of loop learning. Loop learning was first described by the late Chris Argyris, former professor at Yale School of Management and Harvard Business School and considered to be the founder of the field of organizational learning. Since its introduction, loop learning has evolved to encompass three distinct types of learning that can occur within an organization: single-loop learning, double-loop learning, and triple-loop learning (Figure 9).[192]

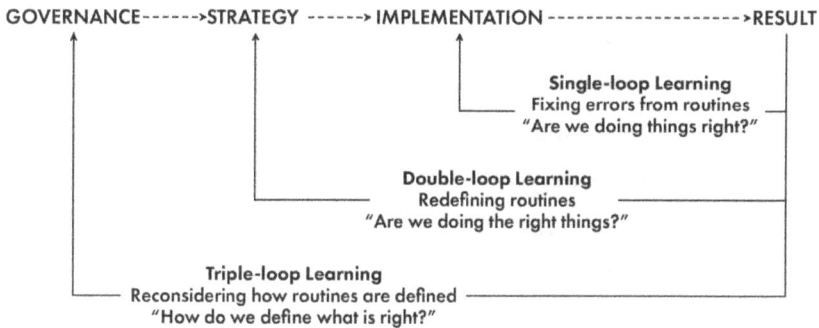

GOVERNANCE------>STRATEGY ------> IMPLEMENTATION ------------------->RESULT

Single-loop Learning
Fixing errors from routines
"Are we doing things right?"

Double-loop Learning
Redefining routines
"Are we doing the right things?"

Triple-loop Learning
Reconsidering how routines are defined
"How do we define what is right?"

Figure 9. Comparing single-, double-, and triple-loop learning.

Single-loop learning is opportunistic, as it refers to refining actions to improve performance without questioning assumptions or established routines.[193] It is the extent of learning achieved within a Planet Simple mindset, as I will explain later on when contrasting adaptive management with incrementalism. Single-loop learning asks: "Are we doing things right?"

Double-loop learning refers to revisiting assumptions underlying cause–effect relationships (e.g., that implementing a specific action such as planting trees will lead to a specific outcome such as greater biodiversity), making adjustments to values and policies, and improving through experimenting with innovative approaches. Double-loop learning asks: "Are we doing the right things?"

To help illustrate, I may offer a comparison of single- and double-loop learning for climate change adaptation. Requests for improved regional climate change models to determine how much to increase the height of dikes or the size of reservoirs represent single-loop learning because the rationale for relying on climate models and as to the suitability of the dike itself are not called into question. Rather, incremental changes are made to established management strategies (often referred to as management levers) by adjusting their height, volume, or quantity (e.g., the dike management lever was simply adjusted upward to a greater height). Double-loop learning, on the other hand, may imply that one takes into account the relocation of dikes, retention areas, and restoration of floodplains rather than simply increasing the height of dikes.[194]

The shift from single- to double-loop learning is the critical shift that corporate sustainability managers need to deliver in order to leave Planet Simple and achieve resilience on Planet Earth. They should also have their eyes on triple-loop learning, although their capacity to achieve it will rely more on system-wide collaboration and change. In triple-loop learning, not only do we think about applying the rules or changing them, we also think about the governance underpinning the rule-making process. Triple-loop learning asks: "How do we decide what is right?"

- - - - - - - - - - - - - - - - - - -

Planet Simple Trap: Adaptive Management or Incrementalism?

This Planet Simple trap distorts adaptive management by reframing it as an incrementalist approach to optimization.

As resilience science gained momentum, so did calls to apply adaptive management. The challenge is that many of the organizations seeking to apply adaptive management have tried to do so while remaining within a Planet Simple mindset. In these instances, adaptive management has been captured by the dominance of Planet Simple, and misinterpreted such that it fails to achieve the double- or triple-loop learning necessary for resilience.

Even on Planet Simple, some degree of learning is likely to occur through experience, although it may be accidental or buried if it uncovers policy failure. The misinterpretation has been that managers claim to be practicing adaptive management simply by changing strategies in response to new information rather than actively designing their management with the goal of learning about uncertainty.[195] Any learning answers the question "Are we doing things right?" (single-loop learning).

This misinterpretation of adaptive management is better known as incrementalism, a "muddling through" model where incremental adjustments to practice are made as experience is accumulated. While some learning inevitably occurs even with incrementalism simply from experience, it is a reactive approach that lacks a purposeful direction with regard to learning about uncertainty and simply reaps whatever benefits derive from earlier experiences.[196] Put another way, it never extends beyond single-loop learning.

Adaptive management, on the other hand, "means much more than simply altering objectives and practices in response to new information; it implies a formal, rigorous approach to management, where activities are treated as opportunities for generating information about the system being managed."[197] Rather than committing itself to the one best way, management becomes truly scientific by treating its strategies as experiments.

Incrementalism, on the other hand, retains management goals of achieving targets or outputs efficiently, without acknowledging the goal of learning through action. When actions are treated as opportunities for generating information, as opposed to delivering the optimal answer demanded by Planet Simple, learning and adaptation become goals of management. Emphasis of appraisal at the back end becomes critical for evaluating performance results and feeding lessons learned into the ongoing decision-making process.[198]

As more corporations seek to understand and manage their nature-related impacts, we are seeing this distortion of adaptive management in the corporate sector. For example, a recent sustainability report published by a multinational maritime services organization suggested that it applies "adaptive management" by monitoring environmental performance and optimizing its working methods as necessary.[199] There is no indication of the uncertainties underlying the corporate strategy, as uncovered through scenario analysis, and how adaptive management is used to help the organization learn and adapt over time. In Part III, we will explore how the right approach to sustainability reporting—the back end of corporate decision-making—can achieve the aims of adaptive management and build the foundation for a resilient organization.

— — — — — — — — — — — — — — — — — — —

True Learning Is Incompatible with Planet Simple

Although many companies will say they are adaptive, achieving organizational learning is fundamentally incompatible with the Planet Simple mindset. This is because a Planet Simple mindset emphasizes comprehensive planning in a quest for certainty prior to decisions (the front end) rather than comprehensive appraisal of outcomes of decisions (the back end). Uncertainties are to be reduced through investing in external research or technology to reach (spurious) certitude before a decision, not through management learning after the decision is made. On Planet Simple, managers are users of knowledge rather than being creators of knowledge as they identify and work through the uncertainties they face. The technically rational decision-making model of Planet Simple emphasizes planning under the assumption that comprehensive research can arrive at the one best way to solve a decision-maker's problem. Appraisal activities, therefore, are deemphasized, as scientific management commits "itself in advance to the correctness and efficacy of its reforms [such that] it cannot tolerate learning of failure."[200]

On Planet Simple, assumptions of certainty in information and stability in the external environment produce the belief that there is no compelling reason for investing in evaluation and reporting beyond what is required for compliance. If any appraisal occurs, it typically focuses on basic monitoring to ensure activities have been implemented as promised rather than whether the activities will actually achieve higher-level outcomes such as increases in biodiversity.[201] Buzz Holling himself found that when efficiency is the overarching goal of management, efforts to monitor performance and anticipate change "withered in competition with internal organizational needs."[202] The end result of deprioritizing appraisal is the inability to learn from action, detect system change, and adapt accordingly.[203]

Adaptive Governance for Planet Earth

In 2010, I was sent to a government agency to understand how they could better integrate climate change into their organizational strategy. Part of my mandate was to help apply resilience thinking and adaptive management, for the reasons outlined in this chapter. Because of the outstanding mentoring I had at that moment in my life, I was encouraged not to go in and immediately take charge. Instead, I was told to observe, collaborate, ask questions, and learn. What I learned was profound and set the stage for the rest of my career (and this book).

The managers I worked with understood the importance of climate change. They understood resilience science and the value of learning from their actions to adapt in the face of uncertainty. Yet they continued to pour their money into project after project, seldom invested in evaluation, and fell prey to the Planet Simple trap of adaptive management as incrementalism. It all clicked for me when one of my collaborators mentioned to me that the organization's spending on monitoring and evaluation could not exceed five percent of its annual budget.

Here it was, in plain sight, an agency trying to implement resilience science within a wider *context* entrenched in Planet Simple thinking. A context organized by command-and-control, that prioritized spending on action over learning, efficiency over resilience. My agency colleagues were never going to succeed, because managing for resilience is fundamentally incompatible with the Planet Simple paradigm they were operating within. Only if we shift from Planet Simple to Planet Earth, and embrace uncertainty in decision-making, will we be able to achieve resilience.

The table below contrasts Planet Simple with Planet Earth. Resilience, as a business objective, is a consequence of adopting a Planet Earth mindset. Attempting to apply resilience within a Planet Simple mindset will result in resilience being distorted according to Planet Simple traps identified throughout this book. There is no mixing and matching—we cannot stay on Planet Simple and achieve resilience.

	PLANET SIMPLE	PLANET EARTH
How We Think the World Works	Stable / Individual / Measurable / Predictable / Linear / Equilibrium	Change / Connected / Complex / Discontinuous / Nonlinear / Tipping points
How We Make Decisions	The world is fully knowable / Certainty is possible	The world is not fully knowable / Uncertainty is always present
Our Business Objectives	Technical rationality / Optimization / Efficiency	Procedural rationality / Robustness / Resilience

And so that brings us to today, where business is expected to manage for resilience within a mindset that remains on Planet Simple. In order for resilience to succeed, the mindset needs to shift as well.

Gunderson mentions how the persistence of Planet Simple thinking results in a distortion of adaptive management away from its original context as a method for understanding and managing complex systems in an ever-changing world.[204] He argues:

Until management institutions are capable and willing to embrace uncertainty and to systematically learn from their actions, adaptive management will not continue in its original context, but will be redefined in a weak context of 'flexibility in decision-making'.[205]

Adaptive governance has been described as the context that enables learning via adaptive management. It is the academic term for the Planet Earth approach to business management that I advocate for in this book. Adaptive governance views knowledge gained through appraisal of on-ground action as critical for harvesting experience and informing decisions. On the other hand, adaptive management is incompatible with the Planet Simple mindset because it does not recognize the potential value of knowledge gained from the bottom-up. Rather, it emphasizes comprehensive planning at the front end (i.e., prior to a decision) under the assumption that uncertainty can be reduced sufficiently for a decision to proceed without the need for monitoring and evaluation.

While proposing adaptive governance as a more suitable paradigm for responding to climate change, experts have observed that many decision-making structures are "still firmly rooted in the tradition of [Planet Simple] management."[206] Despite today's mandates to manage for resilience, Planet Simple management remains intact, as management continues to put its effort at the front end and to emphasize planning over appraisal, as was expected of my colleagues back in 2010.

Will today's calls for business to manage for resilience fall prey to the same traps? Part III offers a practical approach to managing for resilience that can avoid the traps of Planet Simple because it is based on the fundamentals of adaptive governance.

PART III:

Business on Planet Earth

> *A company's ability to generate cash flows is inextricably linked to the interactions between the company and its stakeholders, society, the economy, and the natural environment.*
>
> —International Sustainability Standards Board

In Part I, we defined Planet Simple and how it came to underpin our worldview of nature, society, government, and business. In Part II, we explored how resilience science better describes the reality of Planet Earth, and its fundamental opposition to Planet Simple. We went through the implications for reshaping corporate strategy by acknowledging uncertainty at the front end of decision-making and investing in reporting and evaluation at the back end to support organizational learning. Now, in Part III, we move from theory to practical advice on how to move your organization from Planet Simple to Planet Earth.

Although the principles of resilience science and adaptive governance will stand the test of time, their influence on today's business mindset is only emerging. This book has described how corporate sustainability practice is often distorted by Planet Simple and caught between inflated expectations and disillusionment (i.e. the hype cycle described in chapter 3). This has led to a bewildering array of advice, frameworks, and standards offered to people trying to get a handle on what to do. Part III offers a way forward by grounding recommendations in the fundamentals of corporate value creation (chapter 7), corporate strategy (chapter 8), and corporate reporting (chapter 9). Many of these recommendations have been honed in recent years with colleagues at BWD Strategic—to whom I am grateful for their collaboration and insight.

My focus on fundamentals seeks to offer relevant guidance no matter how future frameworks and regulations unfold. With this said, I will refer to frameworks, documents, and standards in place at the time of writing (2024) so that readers can connect the fundamentals to what they are encountering in their day-to-day. If readers pick up this text at a much later date, the fundamentals should remain relevant but the names of frameworks and standards may have changed.

FURTHER READING

Readers interested in understanding these changes can follow the developments or suggest edits at the companion website for Leaving Planet Simple, dralexgold.com. To visit the site, scan the QR code below:

CHAPTER 7

Value Creation on Planet Earth

> *ESG is the big picture, not just a piece of the puzzle.*
>
> —Bill McNabb, Dennis Carey, and Ram Charan, *Talent, Strategy,*
> *Risk: How Investors and Boards Are Redefining TSR*

Sustainability as Inside-Out Risk

On March 24, 1989, the oil supertanker Exxon Valdez, captained by Joseph Hazelwood, ran aground on the Bligh Reef (yes, named for the same Captain Bligh of "Mutiny on the Bounty Fame") in Prince William Sound off Alaska, spilling 10.8 million gallons into the sea over the next few days. Soon, TV stations around the world broadcasted images of cormorants, goldeneyes, and even bald eagles covered with thick, black oil, struggling to survive. Public outcry naturally ensued. One eventual result, some eight years later, was the founding of the Global Reporting Initiative (GRI) in Boston in 1997. In some ways, it was the birth of the corporate sustainability movement.

GRI had its roots in two nonprofit organizations: CERES (previously known as the Coalition for Environmentally Responsible Economies) and Tellus Institute, an environmental consulting agency founded in 1976. Its aim, as stated on its own website, "was to create the first accountability mechanism to ensure companies adhere to responsible environmental conduct principles, which was then broadened to include social, economic, and governance issues."[207] GRI published its first sustainability reporting guidelines in 2000. Since then, they have evolved into the GRI Standards—the most commonly used sustainability reporting framework in the world.

GRI asked a business to identify its material impacts on environment and society, borrowing the concept of materiality from financial accounting in an attempt to bring rigor to the sustainability disclosure space (but inadvertently setting the stage for major confusion present today, as will be discussed further in this chapter). GRI also acknowledged the relationship between a company's material impacts and financial performance, stating: "material [environmental and social] topics will often have a significant financial impact in the near-term or long-term on an organization."[208]

This acknowledgment was ahead of its time, however, and GRI's mission was quickly distorted by the Planet Simple assumption that sustainability is separate to core business. Companies did not always use the GRI Standards to identify material sustainability issues, reduce their wider impact, and acknowledge the relationship between sustainability context and financial performance. The focus was often on reputation management, preventing highly publicized environmental disasters. No one wanted to be the next Exxon, or Joseph Hazelwood (a modern-day Captain Bligh) for that matter. Corporate sustainability was considered a function of the public affairs team—a Planet Simple trap that remains common today (Figure 10).

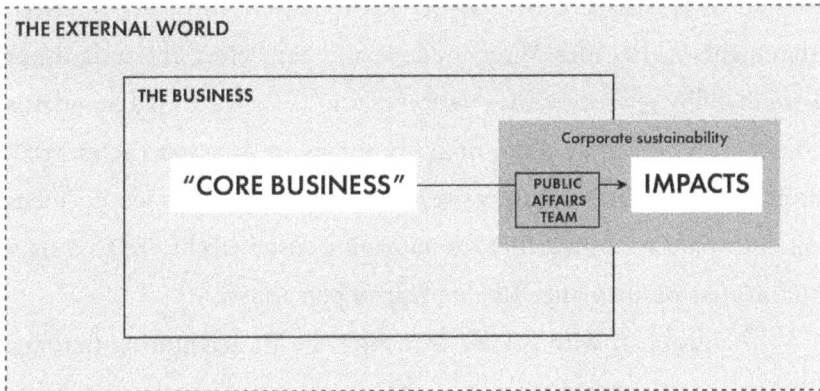

THE EXTERNAL WORLD

THE BUSINESS

Corporate sustainability

"CORE BUSINESS" — PUBLIC AFFAIRS TEAM → IMPACTS

Figure 10. The "inside-out" view of corporate sustainability conceptualizes it as a collection of environmental and social impacts distinct from so-called core business and best managed by the public affairs team for reputational purposes.

While it can be said that GRI Standards drove greater accountability from corporations around the world, they have also supercharged the Planet Simple trap of CSR that we discussed in chapter 2. Corporate sustainability became about managing discrete environmental issues, not understanding corporate value creation within a wider system. The focus was on charity drives, community clean-ups, and other "responsible" initiatives separate to so-called core business. Before too long, for many companies, it was business as usual: no news equals good news.

Sustainability as Outside-In Risk

Then, in 2011, the corporate sustainability movement developed further with the founding of the Sustainability Accounting Standards Board, or SASB.[209] It drew its inspiration from the accounting industry, where the two main standards bodies, the International Accounting Standards Board (IASB) and the US-focused Financial Accounting

Standards Board (FASB), had set standards for company financial statements for decades. Why not develop a parallel set of standards for sustainability reporting, the reasoning went. While the GRI Standards focused on corporate accountability for its impacts on the external world (the *inside-out* perspective), the SASB Standards would focus on corporate accountability for managing sustainability-related risks to business performance (the *outside-in* perspective).

The problem with SASB, drawing from its accounting heritage and its investor perspective, was that it was also distorted by Planet Simple thinking. Corporates and investors used the SASB Standards to characterize sustainability as a collection of isolated risks, just like any other risk that business had to deal with (Figure 11). Sustainability was seen as just one piece of the puzzle, rather than the overarching context within which the business operates.[210] Still, by reporting a few SASB metrics, companies could find themselves attractive candidates for the ESG investing boom that would emerge more recently, as we discussed in chapter 3.

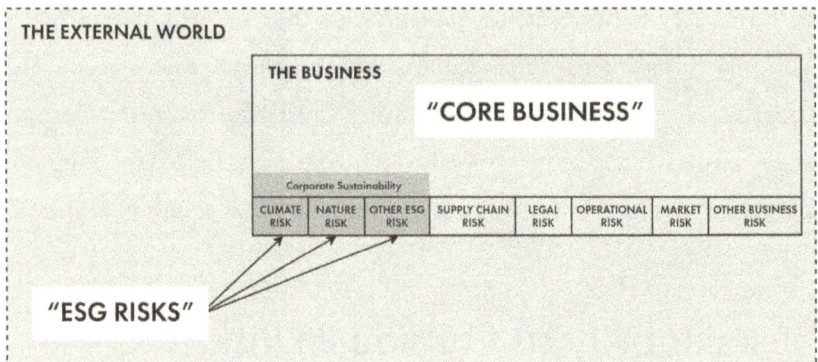

Figure 11. *The outside in-view of corporate sustainability acknowledges that environmental and social issues are relevant for financial performance, but conceptualizes these issues as discrete risks on a similar scale to other business risks.*

▬ ▬ ▬ ▬ ▬ ▬ ▬ ▬ ▬ ▬ ▬ ▬ ▬ ▬ ▬ ▬ ▬ ▬ ▬

Planet Simple Trap: The Double Materiality Matrix

This Planet Simple trap distorts the reality of Planet Earth by characterizing corporate sustainability as a collection of discrete issues that can be measured and prioritized using conventional risk management techniques.

It is common to see businesses trying to understand sustainability from both an outside-in perspective and inside-out perspective by creating a *double materiality* matrix (Figure 12). Double materiality matrices feature axes of:

- Stakeholder impact (the inside-out perspective)
- Impact on the business (the outside-in perspective)

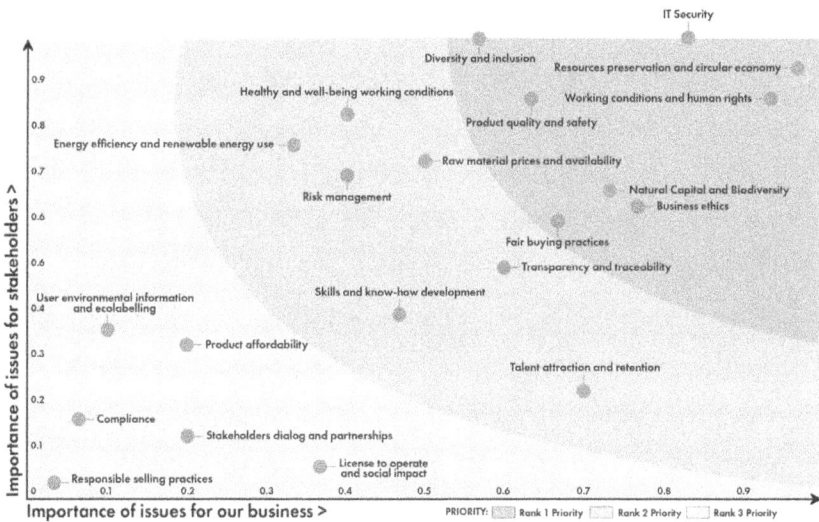

Figure 12. An anonymous example of a double materiality matrix commonly found in corporate sustainability reporting.

It is not hard to see how this is a rather Planet Simple approach to understanding the complexity of corporate sustainability. Carol Adams, now chair of the body that creates the GRI Standards, bemoaned the materiality matrix simplifying "the inherent complexity of assessing material sustainability issues, stakeholder engagement, and the societal pursuit of sustainable development."[211]

Like all the other Planet Simple traps in this book, the materiality matrix represents an attempt to distort the reality of corporate sustainability so it fits into the box supplied by the existing paradigm—which in this case is a risk management matrix supplied by enterprise risk management practice. We didn't really think twice as to whether this was accurate, because as humans "we have a sufficiently strong propensity not only to make divisions in knowledge where there are none in nature, and then to impose the divisions on nature, making the reality thus conformable to the idea."[212]

Does reality actually conform to the matrix, though? A critical look at the reality underpinning any double materiality matrix would suggest otherwise.

First, the matrix represents a misleading illusion of certainty, which although illusory is welcome on Planet Simple (as explained in chapter 5). For example, the matrix forces the user to rank various issues or risks based on their importance or impact. I've often seen diversity and inclusion ranked higher than, say, workplace safety. As an LGBTQ+ person, I have faced anguish in the workplace and will always fight for the importance of diversity and inclusion. But is it more important than my health and safety? Aren't they intertwined?

On the flip side, is an incident of discrimination really more impactful than someone dying on the workroom floor? No one would actually say that an issue like diversity "is about 15 percent more important" than another issue like health and safety, yet this is what the matrix often says. The prioritization in the matrix represents false choices that don't actually reflect how these issues are prioritized strategically. Businesses will do what they need to do to achieve diversity and safety objectives together. As fellow sustainability reporting enthusiast Elaine Cohen wrote:

"I don't think we need to mess around with shades of materiality...high materiality, low materiality, average materiality...What difference do these labels make in terms of management attention, resource allocation, due diligence? All material topics should be assigned the level of resource required to address the need, the relative priority is superfluous to requirements."[213]

In addition to the illusion of order, or relative priority, the matrix offers the illusion of stability. Even if it were true that diversity and inclusion are 15 percent more important than health and safety at the time of the materiality assessment, would it still be 15 percent more important after a series of safety-related incidents? There is also risk here, as the matrix may invite criticism that the company deprioritized health and safety and could have done more to prevent the incidents. Why would any business leader want to open themselves up to that when they know things are always changing in reality?

With change comes uncertainty; and an unbiased appreciation of uncertainty is a cornerstone of rationality, as we discussed in Part II. The spurious certitude of the matrix, like all Planet Simple thinking, fails this test. A more realistic, Planet Earth representation would simply list important issues and disclose how the business managed them through the reporting period.

In summary, sustainability should not be seen as a collection of public affairs issues to manage (like the next Exxon Valdez) or idiosyncratic risks (like workplace safety) to the business. Rather, it represents a transformation of business to acknowledge something that has been true all along—that the enterprise exists within, and depends upon, a wider system (as noted when reviewing the mechanics of system change in chapter 4). So how can we break away from the reductionist Planet Simple traps and manage for holistic value creation?

━ ━ ━ ━ ━ ━ ━ ━ ━ ━ ━ ━ ━ ━ ━ ━ ━ ━

Sustainability as the Context for Corporate Value Creation

In a recent paper titled "The Imperative of Impact Management," the authors wrote:

> A narrow approach to addressing sustainability issues focused solely on the management of entity-specific risks is insufficient, because it is not attuned to rapid environmental and social developments, and importantly, it does not take into account the contributions that enterprises make to the accumulation of system-wide risk, as well as their consequences.[214]

This passage gets at the fundamental distortion that underpins today's commonplace application of both the SASB and GRI Standards. By failing to acknowledge that business operates within a wider system, Planet Simple takes the list of sustainability topics identified by SASB and GRI—GHG emissions, employee diversity, and so on—as simply the next "risks" to consider, on the same scale as other business risk. But climate change and other systemic risks exist at a scale above the enterprise, on a global scale that is interconnected, where the behavior of one enterprise is not isolated but inextricably linked together with those of other enterprises and organizations around the world. The impact of one enterprise, either on the environment or on society, may be considered "low risk" or marginal, but collectively, it could be substantial.

The imperative is not just for individual companies but for the health of the economy and society as a whole. "The systemic nature of the relationship between the economy, people, and the natural environment makes the management of impacts an economic and financial imperative as well."[215]

The solution for characterizing corporate sustainability as value creation within a wider system has been with us for over a decade, but few saw it because it was hidden inside a reporting framework. Few saw it because on Planet Simple, reporting is a burden to be minimized rather than an integral part of strategy development (see chapter 6). With this mindset, why would anyone look in the International Integrated Reporting Framework for a model that helps it integrate sustainability into corporate value creation?

A bit of background will help make the connection between the International Integrated Reporting Framework and corporate value creation. In 2011, the International Integrated Reporting Council (IIRC) published its first Discussion Paper. In it, they made clear their aims: "The IIRC aims to forge a global consensus on the direction in which reporting needs to evolve, creating a framework for reporting that is better able to accommodate complexity, and, in so doing, brings together the different strands of reporting into a coherent, integrated whole."[216]

The paper highlighted how, indeed, the world had changed with globalization and the resulting interdependencies between economies and supply chains, advances in technology, rapid population growth, and increasing global consumption. (This is Planet Earth, but it put the cart before the horse because the Planet Simple world did not recognize the strategic value of a disclosure framework.) If the world had changed so dramatically, then why not change the standards we use to measure, disclose, and appraise corporate performance?

The report also noted a key statistic. That is, in 1975, 83 percent of the market value of the S&P 500 could be explained by measuring simply those firms' financial and physical assets. By 2009, this number had plummeted to just 19 percent and is probably even lower today.[217] Think about it, in 1975, among the largest US companies were Exxon, General Motors, General Electric, Dow Chemical, and Procter & Gamble.[218] They had tangible assets, oil in the ground, sprawling factories, or inventory sitting in warehouses or on the shelves. Fast forward to today and among the top companies are Apple, Microsoft, Google, Amazon, and Meta. Their market value is many multiples of the physical and financial assets they own. The difference: intangible value.

But the IIRC was one of the first to recognize this and, more importantly, propose a framework for understanding the holistic reality of corporate value creation. The framework codified the multi-capital model of corporate value creation, one of the most powerful articulations of how financial success relies on environmental and social capital instead of on financial capital alone (Figure 13).

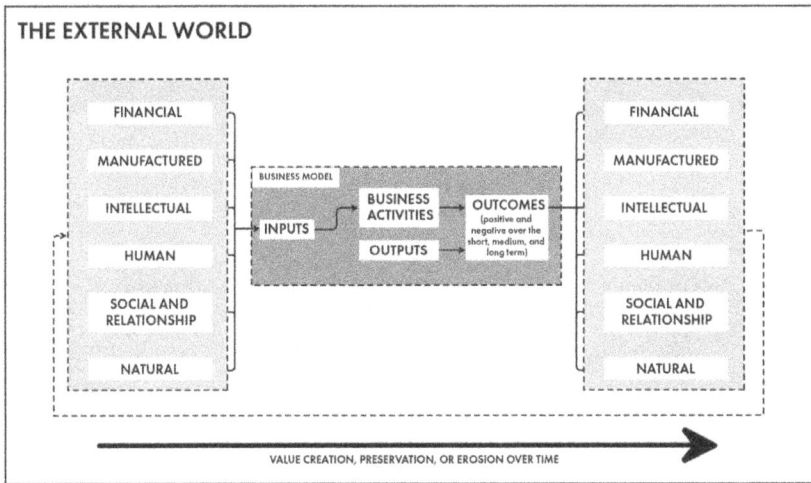

THE EXTERNAL WORLD

FINANCIAL		FINANCIAL
MANUFACTURED		MANUFACTURED
INTELLECTUAL	BUSINESS MODEL	INTELLECTUAL
HUMAN	INPUTS → BUSINESS ACTIVITIES → OUTCOMES (positive and negative over the short, medium, and long term)	HUMAN
	OUTPUTS	
SOCIAL AND RELATIONSHIP		SOCIAL AND RELATIONSHIP
NATURAL		NATURAL

VALUE CREATION, PRESERVATION, OR EROSION OVER TIME →

Figure 13. The multi-capital model of corporate value creation suggests that businesses depend on financial, manufactured, intellectual, human, social, and natural capital to create value. It holds that a business's impacts on these sources of capital can result in financial risks and opportunities over time.

The multi-capital model of corporate value creation offered a way to recognize the environmental and social context of business performance, and measure success through nonfinancial indicators.[219]

Type	Definition
Financial Capital	The traditional yardstick of performance; includes funds obtained through financing or generated by means of productivity.
Manufactured Capital	Encompasses physical infrastructure and related technology, such as equipment and tools.
Human Capital	The knowledge, skills, competencies, and other attributes embodied in individuals that are relevant to economic activity.
Social (and Relationship) Capital	Networks together with shared norms, values, and understandings that facilitate cooperation within or among groups.
Natural Capital	The stock of renewable and non-renewable natural resources (e.g., plants, animals, air, water, soils, minerals) that combine to yield a flow of benefits to people.
Intellectual Capital	The skills and know-how of an organization's personnel, in addition to their commitment and motivation—which affect their ability to fulfill their roles.

IMPLICATIONS FOR "DOUBLE MATERIALITY"

One of the key contributions of the multi-capital model of value creation is the insight that if a company negatively impacts environmental or social capital, it may be eroding the resource base that it depends on to create value over the long term. This reality means that while it may be tempting to characterize sustainability issues as *inside-out* versus *outside-in*, we cannot see these categories as mutually exclusive when it comes to a company's financial performance over the long term.

Recalling a passage from earlier in this chapter, GRI stated that a company's most important impacts on society and the environment "will often have a significant financial impact in the near-term or long-term on an organization."[220] Even EFRAG, who developed the 2023 European Sustainability Reporting Standards (ESRS) widely considered by many to be the beacon of double materiality, stated that companies "may assume that sustainability matters are financially material when they have been assessed to be material from an impact perspective."[221] Put another way, if an "inside-out" business impact is important enough to be "material," then it can be assumed to also be a material "outside-in" effect on business performance. Yet another standard setter acknowledging the Planet Earth reality that sustainability issues cannot be reduced to discrete inside-out and outside-in risks.

In the IFRS Sustainability Disclosure Standards (which will be reintroduced in chapter 9), the International Sustainability Standards Board (ISSB) chose to define value creation with reference to its dependencies and impacts on "resources and relationships" throughout its value chain:

> An entity's ability to generate cash flows over the short, medium and long term is inextricably linked to the interactions between the entity and its stakeholders, society, the economy and the natural environment throughout the entity's value chain. Together, the entity and the resources and relationships throughout its value chain form an interdependent system in which the entity operates. The entity's dependencies on those resources and relationships and its

impacts on those resources and relationships give rise to sustainability-related risks and opportunities for the entity.[222]

Determining What's Material for Value Creation on Planet Earth

So how can we put this into practice? How can we be sure we develop a corporate sustainability strategy appropriate for Planet Earth, rather than falling into the Planet Simple trap of framing sustainability as a collection of *outside-in* and *inside-out* issues separate to core business?

The good news is that the foundations of today's sustainability frameworks are much more aligned than is commonly considered. We just described how GRI, ESRS, and IFRS Sustainability Disclosure Standards are aligned in recognizing the interplay between company impacts and financial performance. So all you need to do is be sure your approach aligns with the evolving standards, rather than relying on preexisting practice or the techniques of peers—both of which may be distorted by Planet Simple. According to today's standards, determining your business's material (i.e., most important) sustainability impacts, risks, and opportunities should include three broad phases:

- Research and engagement

- Identify and assess material matters—your business's most important sustainability-related impacts, risks, or opportunities (which I will refer to as "material matters")

- Identify material information—how you will evaluate and disclose your ongoing management of material matters

RESEARCH AND ENGAGEMENT—
MEGATRENDS ANALYSIS

The quote at the beginning of this chapter—*ESG is the big picture, not just a piece of the puzzle*—embodies the reality that business success is dependent on broader social and environmental conditions. Emerging trends and global challenges present risks and opportunities for an organization's strategy, and social or environmental disruptions can easily foil the most detailed strategic plans. Recognizing the "big picture" reality of corporate sustainability and ESG, your materiality assessment should start with a megatrends analysis—aimed at revealing the global trends that will impact your ability to create value over the short, medium, and long term. A full appreciation of the complexities of your external environment gives confidence to senior decision-makers and other key stakeholders that megatrends—and the material issues that are derived from them—have been properly considered.

Megatrends are "large, transformative global forces that define the future by having far-reaching impacts on business, economies, industries, societies and individuals."[223] Think tanks, universities, governments, nonprofit organizations, industry associations, and consultancies prepare and publish research and analyses on global megatrends. These reports help to identify and highlight new, complex, and unpredictable forces and trends that may impact business, environment, and society.

Your own corporate strategy function may also have done some research into megatrends. Engaging them at this stage of the process would help bring them "inside the tent" on your Planet Earth approach to corporate sustainability (or if they rebuff you because sustainability is separate to "core business," you'll gain valuable insight that they remain stuck on Planet Simple).

It's important to ground the megatrends research in an analysis of your current approach to sustainability. This phase should also include a review of your existing corporate strategy, sustainability approach, and draw upon any other relevant internal/external documentation that you might have available. Examples of useful documents to review include: your latest annual report, your latest sustainability report, recent investor presentations, and recent internal presentations to the executive and/or board on sustainability.

Starting with a megatrends analysis also meets the expectations of every global reporting standard that requires a materiality assessment. This seems to have been forgotten or missed by many materiality assessment processes offered on the market today—many of which start with a review of material issues identified by your peers. Whatever you do, don't start with a peer review. Starting with a review of material issues identified by others has its roots in Planet Simple thinking, where sustainability is framed as a collection of public affairs issues. We will get to a peer review later in our process.

RESEARCH AND ENGAGEMENT— STAKEHOLDER INTERVIEWS

Stakeholder engagement is a critical component of any materiality assessment. Deep-dive interviews with a mix of internal and external stakeholders are essential. Internal interviews should include your most senior executives, and a mix of other managers as resources permit. External stakeholders should include key customers, suppliers, investors, industry associations, and relevant authorities.

The purpose of the interviews should be twofold: (a) perform a strengths, weaknesses, opportunities, threats (SWOT) analysis on your business, and (b) understand the severity of your business's stakeholder impacts.

When performing the SWOT analysis, interviewees should be asked to focus on megatrends most relevant to their job. The World Resources Institute (WRI) has developed a sustainability-specific SWOT tool focused on understanding the SWOT from a corporate sustainability perspective (i.e., impacts, dependencies, and related megatrends).[224]

If your business impacts stakeholders and you wish to align with impact-focused frameworks such as the United Nations Guiding Principles on Business and Human Rights, the ESRS, or the GRI, then it is important to include impacted stakeholders in this phase of engagement. If you are unable to identify or access impacted stakeholders (which may be the case for potential impacts deep in your supply chain, for example), relevant standards may permit the use of credible proxies instead. Credible proxies are individuals with sufficiently deep experience in engaging with affected stakeholders from a particular region or context (e.g., women workers on farms, indigenous peoples, or migrant workers) who can help to effectively convey their likely concerns. In practice, this can include development and human rights NGOs, international trade unions, and local civil society organizations, including faith-based organizations.

You may have noticed that I have recommended that interviews are targeted to focus on SWOT or impact. Some assessment methods suggest more general questions such as "what do you think are the most important sustainability issues facing the business today and into the future?" Leading with general questions like this can lead to poor results because they fail to bring the participant out of Planet Simple. In particular:

- Stakeholders are not asked to focus on their area of expertise and so end up focusing on ill-defined assumptions of what "sustainability" means.

- Stakeholders are not asked to think in terms of the corporate strategy, and so may consider sustainability issues as separate to "core business."

- Answers to questions are more likely to be skewed by one of the many biases plaguing corporate sustainability. For example, if there was an article in the paper about a gender discrimination lawsuit last month, you can bet that every stakeholder will mention the importance of gender diversity (availability bias).[225] This may take up precious interview time to discuss something that your research would have uncovered during the context analysis phase anyway. Without targeted questioning, you may fail to uncover important internal information, such as business plans to invest in a manufacturing facility with a new type of hazardous work.

Many materiality assessments make use of surveys. They can be a useful way to solicit feedback about what's important to people, but they generally are unable to get to the level of depth required to understand the connections between sustainability, your corporate strategy, and external impact. If you have the resources to administer surveys, then they can be deployed as a component of stakeholder engagement but should not be used in the place of deep-dive interviews.

RESEARCH AND ENGAGEMENT— VALUE CHAIN MAPPING

Today's standards require the identification of material matters with reference to the "interdependent system" within which your business operates. Visualizing your business's value chain is a way of bringing this "interdependent system" to life. It provides the foundation for articulating how sustainability-related risks, opportunities, and impacts intersect with your business's value creation strategy.

When identifying sustainability-related risks, opportunities, and impacts, the "value chain" is defined broadly, as the full range of interactions, resources, and relationships related to your business model and your external environment. It encompasses everything your businesses uses and depends on to create its products or services from conception to delivery, consumption, and end of life. It includes:

- Employees and other resources within your "own operations"

- Suppliers that provide products and services used in your own operations (your "upstream value chain")

- Distributors, retailers, customers, waste facilities that receive your products and services (your "downstream value chain")

- The financing, geographical, geopolitical, and regulatory environments in which your business operates (your "external environment")

To articulate how sustainability issues intersect with your value chain, it is useful to think in terms of impact and dependency pathways:

- An impact pathway describes how your business activities, products, and services result in positive or negative changes to specific value chain resources and relationships

- A dependency pathway shows how your business activities depend on inputs sourced from specific value chain resources and relationships

Some questions to help get you started mapping your value chain include:[226]

- What are the resources and relationships, or dependencies, that your business draws upon to create value?

- How do these resources and relationships translate into inputs?

- What are the key activities of your business as it transforms inputs into outputs?

- What is the external environment that your business operates in, the local environment, the regional environment, the national environment, and the global environment?

- What are the trends in those environments that could present risks and opportunities for your business?

The following table explains how value chain dependencies, impacts, and external factors can be associated with financial risks or opportunities.

Value Chain Component	Connection to Enviornmental or Social Factors	Financial Risk or Opportunity
Dependency	The company depends on a highly skilled workforce to achieve its strategy.	Revenue growth may not achieve target if company fails to attract and retain talent. This may have flow-on financial effects associated with investor sentiment, share price, and cost of capital.
Dependency	A small percentage of the company's workforce is unionized.	A failure to uphold freedom of association and collective bargaining can increase expenses and reduce revenue because of work stoppages.
Dependency	The company depends on natural gas in its manufacturing processes.	Fluctuations in availability and pricing of natural gas may increase operating expenditures, reduce margins, reduce performance according to key financial metrics such as EBITDA.
Impact	Employees at the company may experience health and safety impacts from manual labor in manufacturing processes.	Health and safety incidents may cause financial effects such as fines, remediation expenses, and reputation challenges that affect revenue and/or employee retention.
Impact	The company's energy usage, including natural gas, GHG emissions, impacts the global environment through contributing to climate change.	Continued GHG emissions may cause financial effects such as exposure to carbon pricing, investor action to reduce emissions, and/or inability to attract customers focused on reducing their own emissions (including their value chain emissions).
Impact	The company sources materials from industries and countries known to have elevated risk of human rights violations.	Human rights impacts in a company's supply chain may lead to financial effects such as fines, sanctions, and reputational effects on revenue.
External Environment	Policy and market factors may cause the availability of fossil fuels to decrease into the future.	In addition to financial risks associated with energy availability, transition away from oil may reduce the availability (and increase the price) of petroleum-based derivatives used as feedstocks in many manufacturing processes.
External Environment	Customer interest in reducing GHG emissions.	Shifting customer preferences toward low-emissions solutions presents an opportunity for the company to develop products and services that avoid or remove GHG emissions from customer operations.
External Environment	Increasing frequency and severity of extreme weather poses increasing threat to business continuity.	Increased extreme weather risk may result in increased expenditure to prepare assets and facilities and pose increased risk of business disruption that may result in revenue loss, staff injury, and property damage.

IDENTIFY AND ASSESS MATERIAL
MATTERS—IDENTIFICATION

Once you've assessed megatrends and operating context, and mapped the value chain, you will be in a good position to generate a "long list" of potential sustainability-related risks and opportunities that may affect your business's prospects. It is important to think broadly here, which is why it is referred to as a "long list." You'll have a chance to focus on the most significant matters once you've assessed impacts, risks, and opportunities for severity or magnitude.

When creating the long list, keep the following in mind:

- *Focus on Plausibility:* The objective of this stage in the process is to canvass any environmental or social factor that could plausibly affect business prospects, based on your under-standing of the business model and value chain. You'll have a chance to prioritize matters later in the assessment process. Including as many matters as plausible allows for this list to become a useful baseline for any future reassessment.

- *Describe Impacts, Risks, and Opportunities with Precision*: You may be familiar with materiality assessments that phrase matters in terms such as "GHG emissions," "health and safety," "public policy," and so on. These assessments remain aligned with the Planet Simple thinking that corporate sustainability is about defining a list of "issues" to manage on the side. In order to get to Planet Earth, we need to do a better job of connecting these issues to corporate value creation. Instead of defining the matter as "GHG emissions," we want to be clear that GHG emissions increase the possibility of financial effects associated with carbon pricing, investor action, and shifting customer preferences. Instead of "health and safety," we want to be clear about the potential impacts to employees across specific business activities, and how these may give rise to financial effects on the business.

- *Identify the Financial or Stakeholder Effect That Will Be Assessed:* In the next phase of the process, we will assess the potential impacts, risks, and opportunities in accordance with best practice assessment frameworks. The assessment won't work if we are asked to assess the severity of stakeholder "impact" and the magnitude of financial "effects"; instead, we should clarify "impacts" and "effects" relevant to assess for each matter. Employees may be impacted by exposure to hazardous materials, which is something that we can assess for severity. The business may face additional future expenditures from carbon pricing, which is something that we can assess for magnitude.

IDENTIFY AND ASSESS—PEER REVIEW AND INVESTOR INTERESTS

As a final step ahead of the assessment phase, it's not a bad idea to compare the issues identified in your draft shortlists with the material issues of your peers. Global standards also suggest considering industry practice when identifying material matters.[227] It's best to conduct this review at the conclusion of your research and engagement phase. This can protect against the tendency to simply replicate industry norms or slightly rephrase issues selected by a respected peer.

There are now several outside sources who have compiled (anonymous) data on sustainability-related issues that you can use in your peer review. One good example is the ESG Navigator tool, which is licensed by The Conference Board and used by nearly one hundred Fortune 500 companies to benchmark and progress their own sustainability strategies. ESG Navigator is also the most cost-effective way to consider the interests of nearly every ESG rating framework used by investors.[228]

IDENTIFY AND ASSESS—ASSESS FOR SEVERITY, MAGNITUDE, AND LIKELIHOOD

Each impact, risk, and opportunity should be assessed using verifiable and transparent methodologies. A good starting point is to assess the severity of potential negative impacts (or benefit of potential positive impacts), as well as their likelihood. Financial risks and opportunities should be assessed for magnitude and likelihood. If your organization has an existing approach to prioritizing risks and opportunities, it can be integrated into your assessment.

Some principles to keep in mind:

- Don't fall prey to the false precision of quantification (expected on Planet Simple), qualitative assessments of severity and/or magnitude are important starting points and may be all that is needed to gain agreement among stakeholders.[229]

- It is often easier to assess impacts, risks, and opportunities through ranking their severity or magnitude relative to each other. Relative rankings offer a useful sense-check that can be performed after the initial assessment of each impact, risk, or opportunity on its own.

- Because of the forward-looking nature of assessing material impacts, risks, and opportunities, the need to rely on judgment is inevitable. Although judgment can be challenging to verify, it would also be inappropriate to force false precision on "measuring" judgment. It is best to gain an agreed judgment across management through transparency, and evolving the judgment over time as management learns from its actions (the adaptive management approach described in chapter 6).

When the assessment is complete, you may wish to group material matters into categories to help with integration into strategy and reporting.

IDENTIFY AND ASSESS—EXECUTIVE VALIDATION

To finalize the materiality assessment process, it's important to gather your team together to validate the material issues identified. In order to determine which issues are material, you will need to agree on the threshold for materiality (a requirement of some reporting standards). Although this threshold is subjective (because it relates to judgments about forward-looking issues), you will want to make sure that the outcomes are verifiable and transparent. In addition to seeking executive sign-off on material impacts, risks, and opportunities, this validation workshop looks to gain buy-in on the integration of these matters into corporate strategy and disclosure.

IDENTIFY MATERIAL INFORMATION

Once your list of material impacts, risks, and opportunities is finalized, it's important to start thinking about how you will report on progress to investors and other stakeholders. This means aligning your list of material impacts, risks, and opportunities to applicable disclosure requirements of relevant reporting standards. This will make a start toward identifying the material information to include in your public disclosure.

To help clarify:

- Identifying material impacts, risks, and opportunities is a *strategic* question: "What are my most important environmental and social impacts, risks, and opportunities?"

- Identifying material information is a *reporting* question: "What information is relevant to investors and other stakeholders regarding my performance in managing my significant impacts, risks, and opportunities?"

The following table illustrates how environmental and social factors in a company's value chain may lead to material financial risks or opportunities, and the material information that would be appropriate to disclose.

Value Chain Connection to Environmental or Social Factors	Financial Risk or Opportunity	Material Information
The company depends on a highly skilled workforce to achieve its strategy.	Revenue growth may not achieve target if company fails to attract and retain talent. This may have flow-on financial effects associated with investor sentiment, share price, and cost of capital.	Workforce-related policies and action plans Employee headcount Employee diversity Turnover rate and new hires Training and development metrics
A small percentage of the company's workforce is unionized.	A failure to uphold freedom of association and collective bargaining can increase expenses and reduce revenue because of work stoppages.	Policies and action plans regarding freedom of association and collective bargaining Number/percent of workforce unionized Work stoppage incidents
The company depends on natural gas in its manufacturing processes.	Fluctuations in availability and pricing of natural gas may increase operating expenditures, reduced margins, reduced performance according to key financial metrics such as EBITDA.	Energy-related policies and action plans, including activities to transition away from natural gas (if applicable) Energy used, broken down by fuel type Percent of expenses spent on energy
Employees at the company may experience health and safety impacts from manual labor in manufacturing processes.	Health and safety incidents may cause financial effects such as fines, remediation expenses, and reputation challenges that affect revenue and/or employee retention.	Workforce safety-related policies and action plans Types of health and safety impacts and risks across the business Safety incident numbers, rates Fatality numbers, rates Lost time numbers, rates Fines/penalties associated with safety incidents Safety observations, near misses, other leading indicators

Value Chain Connection to Environmental or Social Factors	Financial Risk or Opportunity	Material Information
The company's energy usage, including natural gas, GHG emissions, which impacts the global environment through contributing to climate change.	Continued GHG emissions may cause financial effects such as exposure to carbon pricing, investor action to reduce emissions, and/or inability to attract customers focused on reducing their own emissions (including their value chain emissions).	Energy efficiency, renewable energy, other emissions-related policies and action plans GHG emissions in own operations (Scope 1 and 2) GHG emissions across the value chain (Scope 3) Capex/opex dedicated to reducing emissions into the future Potential emissions-related expenses that the company may need to pay in the future (e.g., carbon tax)
The company sources materials from industries and countries known to have elevated risk of human rights violations.	Human rights impacts in a company's supply chain may lead to financial effects such as fines, sanctions, and reputational effects on revenue.	Human rights policies and action plans, including due diligence, remediation, and grievance mechanisms Number and results of human rights audits completed Human rights-related complaints or violations, and any associated fines/penalties
Customer interest in reducing GHG emissions.	Shifting customer preferences toward low-emissions solutions presents an opportunity for the company to develop products and services that avoid or remove GHG emissions from customer operations.	R&D activities focused on product innovation to low-emissions solutions Expenditure on low-emissions R&D Number/percent of sales of low-emissions products Customer satisfaction with low-emissions products
Increasing frequency and severity of extreme weather poses increasing threat to business continuity.	Increased extreme weather risk may result in increased expenditure to prepare assets and facilities, and pose increased risk of business disruption that may result in revenue loss, staff injury, and property damage.	Extreme weather policies and action plans, including activities to prepare for increasing severity of extreme weather Capex/opex invested in enhancing preparedness Value of losses (or other financial consequences) incurred from extreme weather

Frequency of Materiality Assessments

On Planet Simple, materiality assessments were reactive. Their results depended on whatever stakeholders considered to be "important" on a given day, and so there was a perception that assessments needed to be revamped regularly to be sure that companies weren't caught out.

On Planet Earth, materiality assessments are simply part of good corporate strategy—helping the business understand the risks, opportunities, and impacts relevant for how it creates value. Any reassessment of your material matters, therefore, should occur in line with your corporate strategic planning process, or if there has been a major change in your business activities.

While reassessing your material matters doesn't need to necessarily happen every year, reassessing the material information about these matters *should* occur every year. This is because the material information will inform the contents of your annual reporting, which needs to be updated every year in accordance with company performance (see the following table for an example of how material impacts, risks, opportunities, and material information may change as business conditions change).

On Planet Earth, business success is inextricably linked with environmental and social factors. By taking the steps in this chapter to acknowledge the context within which your business creates value, you are ready to take the next step and integrate them into your company's strategic planning and governance.

	Material Impacts, Risks, Opportunities	Material Information
Year 1	Materiality assessment identifies the potential for employee injury in manufacturing as a material impact on employees and a material financial risk.	Material information related to this material matter in Year 1 may include: • Policies, procedures, and action plans related to manufacturing safety • Metrics and targets related to manufacturing safety.
Year 2—there is an employee fatality at the company's manufacturing site	The fatality does not change the assessment that employee injury is a material impact and risk.	The fatality does change the material information relevant for the material matter in Year 2. In addition to the information from Year 1, the material information in Year 2 may include: • Information on the fatality, how it occurred, and any remediation or improvements put in place since • Regulatory penalties relevant to the incident • Any legal action that the company may be subject to.
Year 3—no fatalities	Material impact/risk of employee injury in manufacturing remains unchanged.	Material information more likely to resemble Year 1; however, there may be a need to disclose the progress of any corrective action plans, regulatory/legal action that continues related to the fatality.
Year 4—business makes a strategic acquisition of a product involving the use of hazardous materials	The presence of hazardous materials is new, and so the material impacts and risks are updated to include employee injury from exposure to hazardous materials (in addition to existing risks associated with manufacturing activity).	Material information would need to be added related to: • Policies, procedures, and action plans related to the handling of hazardous materials • Metrics and targets related to hazardous materials.

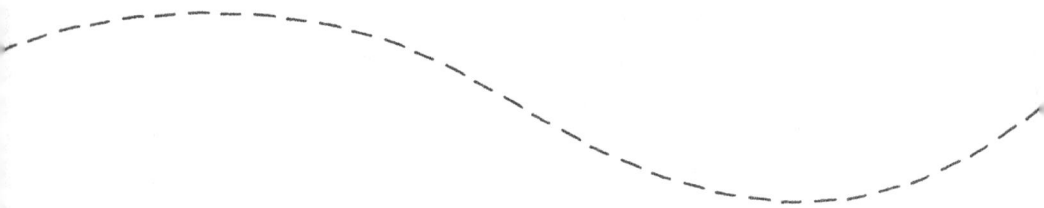

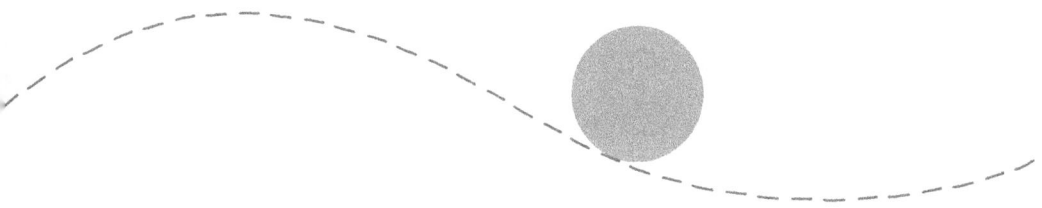

CHAPTER 8

Strategy on Planet Earth

> *No matter how well we prepare ourselves, when the imagined future becomes the very real present, it never fails to surprise.*
>
> —Alan AtKisson, *Believing Cassandra*

In the previous chapter, we discussed value creation on Planet Earth and how you can conduct a materiality assessment to better understand your business's most important sustainability-related impacts, risks, and opportunities. That sets the stage for this chapter, where we discuss strategy on Planet Earth. To get started, we will ask: what are we trying to achieve?

Setting Objectives Using a Theory of Change

On Planet Simple, corporate sustainability is about reputation and "good news" stories (refer back to the Planet Simple trap of CSR from chapter 2). The success of Planet Simple sustainability is measured in dollars spent (or donated) or activities completed. These are enough to get the headlines and allow the rest of the company to get back to "core business."

There is also a hypocrisy at play here. Planet Simple businesses will claim that they *care* about environmental and social outcomes, but many of us know that dollars spent and activities completed may not actually generate real outcomes. A company may spend millions on training activities, but participants report no real change in behavior. Money is spent on health benefits only to have participants not use them fully. The hypocrisy here is that businesses seem more interested in receiving credit for making the effort instead of achieving the intended outcome. They *care* more about their own reputation than the outcome they claim to have on people or the environment.

At the same time, businesses are for-profit entities that shouldn't be expected to step in where the public sector is dropping the ball. Leaving Planet Simple will help businesses focus their sustainability objectives on material risks and opportunities (as described in chapter 7). These risks and opportunities are defined with reference to their strategy and business model, not with reference to what they should *care* about as defined by the moral or political winds of the day.

This should be a sigh of relief for readers thinking I was going to suggest every business find a way to incorporate the outcomes of ending poverty or reversing nature loss into core business. Not quite. Once we make the connection between environmental and social issues and value creation, however, we can articulate how our sustainability strategy supports our corporate strategy. To help set meaningful objectives for our sustainability strategy, we should focus on the stakeholder outcomes and business benefit we hope to achieve through our funding and actions. To do this, we should use methods commonly referred to as *theory of change* or *outcome mapping*.[230]

These methods differentiate between:

- Inputs: Resources (time, money, people-hours) invested by the company

- Outputs: Activities completed or products sold

- Outcomes: The change experienced by stakeholders and/or the business, attributable to the outputs[231]

Inputs (Well Understood on Planet Simple)	Outputs (Well Understood on Planet Simple)	Stakeholder Outcomes (Poorly Understood on Planet Simple)	Business Outcomes (Poorly Understood on Planet Simple)
Number of employees	Diversity of workforce Number of diversity-related activities completed	Inclusive culture Employee psychological safety	Increased engagement Increased productivity Wider pool of applicants
Operational expenses on energy	Energy used Number of energy efficiency projects	GHG emissions Emissions reductions from energy efficiency projects	Expenses avoided from energy efficiency projects Reduced risks from carbon pricing
Charitable donations	Number of charity programs supported	Community outcomes such as reduced hunger, reduced homelessness	Increased employee engagement Increased social license to operate

On Planet Simple, focusing on inputs and outputs was sufficient because sustainability was not considered to have any meaningful connection to business benefit. Furthermore, spurious certitude enabled business to assume their activities would automatically lead to the intended outcomes (refer to chapter 5 for more on spurious certitude and corporate decision-making). In a more practical sense, businesses have resisted setting outcome-oriented objectives because realizing these objectives often involves factors outside of the business's control. Realizing profits also involves factors outside of the business's control and this has not stopped businesses from issuing profit guidance to investors. Along with this guidance, however, management will present important uncertainties and assumptions. The same rigor can be applied to a company's sustainability objectives.

Apart from connecting inputs and outputs to outcomes, theory of change methods allow management to articulate key assumptions. Without identifying outcomes and articulating underlying assumptions, companies remain stuck on Planet Simple and risk greenwash and wasted effort. Achieving the outcomes of a health benefits program may assume that employees are aware of the program and its benefits are easily accessible. Achieving the outcomes of a reforestation project may assume that the organization implementing the project is well-run and not dealing with corrupt political regimes. Identifying assumptions is the first step toward true adaptive management and organizational learning, as described in chapter 6.

Once you've set your desired outcomes and identified key assumptions, it's time to test the uncertainties underlying your strategic direction using scenario analysis.

Scenario Analysis

If you've been following along in Part III, you would have identified sustainability impacts, risks, and opportunities related to your value creation strategy. You've set a level of ambition regarding sustainability outcomes and identified key uncertainties. It's now time to build resilience into your way forward.

As introduced in chapter 5, scenario analysis is a useful tool for building a strategy robust to future uncertainties. Scenario analysis helps expand thinking about what the future may hold and encourages the testing of alternative action plans.

Our discussion will focus on climate scenario analysis because there is well-developed guidance. Guidance has been published for nature-related scenario analysis[232] and emerging standards have suggested that companies should perform scenario analysis for any of their material risks and opportunities.[233]

TYPES OF SCENARIO ANALYSIS

Relevant guidance suggests three types of scenario analysis, as summarized in the following table.

Type of Scenario Analysis	Description	Suitability
Qualitative storylines	Consideration of storylines of change against low-emissions (transition) scenarios and high-emissions scenarios. Useful starting point if participants are unclear of how climate may affect the business at all. Usually not specific enough to meet requirements of emerging standards.	All companies
Customized scenario analysis, using qualitative and quantitative information	Development of scenarios customized to the business, based on publicly available scenario archetypes. Quantification where data and methods allow. Enables enough precision to inform strategy, risk management, and ongoing reporting. Able to be completed by any company without undue cost or effort.	All companies
Scenario analysis using bespoke modeling	Development of bespoke climate and/or financial models to gain increasing levels of granularity about potential future change. Suitable when customized scenarios using publicly available scenario archetypes reveal matters that could significantly impact the business, requiring further investigation. Expanded modeling efforts may increase risks of false precision. Black box models may result in information that does not meet principles of verifiability and auditability.	Emissions-intensive industries

Our focus in this book will be the customized scenario analysis using qualitative and quantitative information. This level of scenario analysis would offer value for any company and is expected to meet emerging requirements for the level of scenario analysis that can be completed without undue cost or effort.[234] Many companies have found this level of scenario analysis to have enough sophistication to inform strategic planning and risk management, while also being straightforward enough to mitigate risks of false precision and poor verifiability.

SCOPING THE CLIMATE-RELATED ISSUES TO INCLUDE IN YOUR SCENARIOS

Scenario analysis will be most effective when it is designed to address your material climate-related risks and opportunities. Some people may perceive a chicken-and-egg issue here because scenario analysis is often described as a way for companies to identify climate-related risks and opportunities. If we need scenario analysis to identify our risks and opportunities, how can we design the process around our risks and opportunities in the first place?

The way I like to think of this is that we use our materiality assessment (as described in chapter 7) to identify how climate may affect our business model *right now*. Scenario analysis is about exploring how the interplay between climate and our business model may evolve *into the future*.

The following table lists climate-related issues that would be suitable for inclusion in a scenario analysis for a car manufacturer compared with a real estate owner and property manager.

Types of Climate-Related Issues	Car Manufacturer	Real Estate Owner and Property Manager
Risks and opportunities associated with the transition to a low-carbon economy (transition risks and opportunities)	• Carbon pricing legislation • Electric vehicle policies and trends	• Carbon pricing legislation • Building energy efficiency regulations • Exposure to fossil fuel tenants
Risks and opportunities associated with extreme weather (acute physical risks/opportunities) or longer-term climate change (chronic physical risks/ opportunities)	• Extreme weather impacts on business continuity • Longer-term population shifts and market demand	• Extreme weather impacts on property damage • Longer-term changes to local building codes as areas become hotter and drier

The above table is not meant to provide an exhaustive list, but rather to illustrate why it is important to scope your important climate-related issues prior to building your scenarios. For example:

- Both the car manufacturer and real estate company emit greenhouse gases (GHGs), so both may be exposed to carbon pricing and so it would make sense to explore carbon pricing developments in each company's scenario analysis.

- For the car manufacturer, it will be important to explore developments in electric vehicle policies and trends, so that it can take advantage of any opportunities for increased usage of its products. Exploring developments in electric vehicles would be less useful for the real estate company, which would benefit more from exploring developments in building energy efficiency regulations in its scenario analysis.

- The real estate company may earn rent revenue from tenants involved in fossil fuel extraction. Some climate scenarios involve significant reduction in fossil fuel production, which would be an important factor to consider in a scenario analysis for the real estate company—given the potential for reduced fossil fuel production to threaten the viability of the real estate company's current tenant base. This consideration would be less relevant to include in the scenario analysis for the car manufacturer.

- Moving to physical risk, both the car manufacturer and the real estate company are exposed to impacts from extreme weather events. For the car manufacturer it would be useful to explore how extreme weather may disrupt production, leading to revenue loss. For the real estate company, on the other hand, it would be useful to explore how extreme weather may damage its properties. It would also be useful to explore how longer-term climate change may increase flood risk over time at sites, potentially reducing property valuations and thus the financial position of the company over time. This would be less of a factor for the financial position of the car manufacturer (unless the car manufacturer also owned the properties and land it uses for production).

BUILDING THE SCENARIOS

Once we've confirmed the climate-related issues we should include in our analysis (usually five to ten issues are sufficient), we should build scenarios that test our assumptions about how these issues will develop into the future. We "build" scenarios by identifying plausible climate-related changes and developments that could happen in the future. Climate-related changes are changes to climate conditions, and climate-related developments are policy, technology, and market developments that may occur.

Climate scenarios can be categorized with reference to the increase of global average temperatures by 2100 (compared to preindustrial) assumed in the scenario. For context, as of 2018, the Earth has warmed by 1°C and emissions continue to grow.[235]

Climate scenarios that assume an increase of 4°C or more by 2100 tend to build in assumptions of unabated emissions, breakdown of existing emissions reduction initiatives, or the crossing of irreversible tipping points. Climate scenarios that assume an increase of under 2°C by 2100 tend to assume increasingly stringent emissions reduction measures, successful emissions-reducing technologies (including carbon capture and storage), and international coordination to meet the aims of the Paris Agreement.[236] Many scenarios land somewhere in the middle. As I will describe later, the best of these scenarios adds to the analysis by offering novel situations or shock events to test the resilience of a company strategy.

At a minimum, you should build two scenarios—one where climate change continues relatively unabated (e.g., 4°C or more by 2100) and another one where decarbonization efforts are successful in meeting the aims of the Paris Agreement (e.g., under 2°C by 2100). The reason for these scenarios is that the 4°C scenario will test your strategy against challenging but plausible physical risks (risks associated with physical impacts of climate change), and the under 2°C scenario will test your strategy against challenging but plausible transition risks (risks associated with the transition to a low carbon economy.[237]

Remember that your scenarios should be customized to explore the climate-related issues of interest to your company. Publicly available scenarios will have useful information, but they are comprehensive datasets that will require some fine-tuning to be useful for your purposes. It is useful to think of these public scenarios as scenario *archetypes* that offer the building blocks for you to use as you build your custom scenarios.[238]

When building scenarios, remember the following principles:

- *Plausible:* To be plausible, the series of events described should be possible, believable, and reasonable within the boundaries of a scenario's architecture, temperature outcome, and overall context. Using scenario archetypes from reputable sources helps achieve plausibility because these archetypes are grounded in comprehensive research and plausible narratives of future possibilities.

- *Challenging:* To be challenging, scenarios should confront conventional wisdom and simplistic understandings of today's environment. They should explore assumptions that will significantly alter the basis for business-as-usual thinking. My recommendation to focus on a high physical risk scenario (i.e., 4°C) and a high transition risk scenario (i.e., under 2°C) aligns with this guidance exploring the upper bounds of what is plausible within the architecture of each climate-related scenario by exploring more severe or confronting potential events that could play out in the future. Considering less challenging scenarios may not adequately test the resilience of your strategy and business models.

- *Coherent and internally consistent:* When scenarios combine information from various archetypes, it is important that the scenario still follows a clear and logical narrative. If we borrow carbon pricing assumptions and GDP projections from different sources for our under 2°C scenario, for example, we need to be sure the ensuing cause and effect remains logical.

Finally, remember from chapter 5 that *consequence*, rather than *likelihood*, is the factor to judge scenarios by. Rather than focusing on the most likely future, our analysis should focus on the most consequential futures (regardless of likelihood)—so long as the analysis remains plausible, challenging, and coherent.

Planet Simple Trap: The Most Likely Scenario

This Planet Simple trap distorts scenario analysis by prioritizing scenarios by likelihood rather than consequence.

You may hear scenario analyses criticized because they don't identify a *most likely* scenario.[239] If you have gotten this far in the book, you should know it is a fool's errand to try to land on a *most likely* scenario of what the world will be in 2030, 2050, or 2100 (if you need a refresher, please revisit chapter 5). It is unsurprising that these criticisms usually come from investors, who generally remain wedded to trying to integrate the challenge of climate change into their reductionist financial analyses—instead of adapting their financial analyses to the reality of climate change (see chapter 3).

While the most likely scenario will help investors get a number to put in their Planet Simple financial analysis, it will most likely (pun intended) set up your corporate strategy for spurious certitude. Identifying a most likely scenario is a Planet Simple trap couched in the assumption that we need to manage for optimization, rather than for resilience. Neither the TCFD nor any subsequent guidance says that companies should identify a most likely scenario when performing a scenario analysis.[240]

Sticking to the principles described in this chapter (and in chapter 5) will help avoid this trap. Earlier I mentioned how scenarios should include at least a low-emissions (e.g. 2°C by 2100) and high-emissions (e.g. 4°C by 2100) scenario. A third scenario that lands somewhere between the low-emissions and high-emissions scenario can be helpful but should include a shock event or similar.

Shock events are important to include in third scenarios because of the tendency for people to gravitate to the *central case* scenario as a *most likely* scenario. Without a shock event, the third scenario becomes a *middle-ground* scenario that seems like an average of the low-emissions and high-emissions scenario. Participants will gravitate to this *central case* as the one to plan for because it seems to address both of the more extreme scenarios at least somewhat.

The opposite is true. Planning for a middle-ground scenario with no shock event ends up addressing neither the low-emissions nor the high-emissions scenario at all. Remember that it is the extremes that cause impact, and ignoring the extremes in favor of the central case is not the recipe for resilience.

IDENTIFYING BUSINESS IMPACT

Once you've built your scenarios, it's time to connect climate-related changes and developments to business impacts. The multi-capital model of value creation (explained in chapter 7) presents a useful starting point. Climate change is more than an environmental impact, and the multi-capital model enables you to identify the various ways climate change may affect your capacity to create value. Apart from helping categorize climate-related issues, the multi-capital model can facilitate the integration of climate-related issues into roles and responsibilities across the organization (see the discussion of integrating sustainability to everyone's job later in this chapter).

The following table shows some examples of how climate-related business impacts can be identified using the multi-capital model of corporate value creation.

Type of Resource (Capital)	Examples of Climate-Related Issues
Money available to the company, cost of capital, investor sentiment (financial capital)	• Divestment from companies with elevated climate risk • Access to sustainability-linked bonds for strong climate performers
Properties, plant, equipment (manufactured capital)	• Physical damage to buildings and equipment • Stranded asset risk • Longer-term climate change shifts conditions outside of current equipment operating limits • Increased insurance premiums for facilities located in high-risk areas
Patents, rights, licenses, internal policies and procedures (intellectual capital)	• Reduced revenue from patents, rights, and licenses from emissions-intensive activities • Existing technologies and management practices become outdated—must be revised to account for climate change • Opportunities to develop new patents to support customers' climate-related objectives
Employees (human capital)	• Health and safety impacts from extreme weather and longer-term weather changes • Poor climate reputation impacts talent attraction and retention
Customers, suppliers, industry and government relationships (social and relationship capital)	• Reduced customer demand for emissions-intensive products and services • Loss of government and industry partnerships if climate objectives are not aligned • Exposure to supplier GHG emissions • Supply chain disruption from extreme weather
Energy, water, air, natural resources and materials (natural capital)	• Changing production costs because of changes to resource pricing • Increased costs to company through carbon taxes, cap and trade schemes, carbon border adjustments

---

Planet Simple Trap: Aggregating Climate Risk

This Planet Simple trap results in bad decisions because it tries to collapse the complexity of climate risk into a single metric that can be prioritized against other business risks.

It is good practice for scenario analysis to consider a range of *perils*—heatwave, storms, sea level rise, and so on—when assessing the physical risks to assets and operations from climate change. They go astray when wedded to the Planet Simple assumption that climate change is a measurable and discrete risk, separate from other business risks. These lead to the assumption that decision-makers need to have a singular climate risk score so that it can be prioritized relative to other risks.

These assumptions lead to a textbook Planet Simple trap. Consider the exposure ratings for a range of climate perils for two sites described in the table below.

Climate Peril	Site A	Site B
Storm	3—Moderate	5—Severe
Heatwave	3—Moderate	5—Severe
Wildfire	3—Moderate	1—Very Low
Sea level rise	3—Moderate	1—Very Low
Drought	3—Moderate	1—Very Low
"Climate risk" at the site (taken as an average)	3	2.6

Busy decision-makers looking for the *answer* and seeking to simplify the climate challenge will prioritize investment in Site A over Site B based on the average climate risk score. Is this the right call?

Probably not. The storm and heatwave risk at Site B are more concerning, given how impact can increase exponentially with severity.

Furthermore, the impacts from storm and heatwave are independent of the other perils. But the averaging suggests that the lack of sea level rise at Site B somehow makes the potential impact from heatwave less. This is flat out wrong—no one would say that the heatwave impact is lessened by the lack of sea level rise—but this is what the average "climate risk" implies.

It may be messier in the short term to consider each peril on its own instead of arriving at an aggregate score, but it is a better approach for the reality of Planet Earth. Avoiding the temptation to aggregate perils also helps characterize climate risk as a driver of existing risks, which we will discuss later in this chapter.

IDENTIFYING FINANCIAL CONSEQUENCES

Once the business impacts have been identified, we need to make the leap to financial performance. The fundamentals of TCFD involve articulating how climate-related issues affect company financials—variables such as revenues, expenses, asset values, cost of capital, and so on. For every climate-related issue identified, you should work with your colleagues to gain a common understanding of how issues may affect financial outcomes (or are already affecting financial outcomes). Defining these *financial impact pathways* lays the groundwork for integration into strategic planning and alignment with financial reporting. For example:

- Increased frequency of drought → reduces water availability for the business → increases operational expenditure on water.

- Increased severity of extreme weather → increased repairs and downtime → reduced productivity/revenue and increased expenditure on facilities/insurance.

- National policies to reduce emissions result in a carbon price → increasing operating expenditure and reduced margins.

The minimum requirement for TCFD and related standards is a qualitative description of how climate-related issues may affect financial performance. According to the TCFD, quantification is appropriate where data and methodologies allow.[241] For example, if a scenario considers a future carbon price range of $10–$20 per ton of CO_2e in 2030 and you estimate your 2030 emissions to be one million tons of CO_2e, you could estimate a range of financial effects from carbon pricing as $10–$20 million in 2030.

This may seem a simple example, but it is important to remember that quantification should be verifiable and not subject to substantial assumptions that limit its usefulness. The TCFD itself noted that it "is not asking organizations to provide a financial forecast (for which scenario analysis is not appropriate). Organizations are asked to provide an indication of direction or ranges of potential financial implications."[242] Businesses may ignore this advice in search of *the answer*, and employ black box methods that obscure important uncertainties. Furthermore, forecasts on their own can fail to inform decision-makers as to the underlying factors that determine financial effects—and this information is vital to designing a strategy for addressing the effects in the first place.

Planet Simple Trap: Substituting Means for Ends in Climate Scenario Analysis

On Planet Simple, the global climate is a new challenge, akin to the rise of terrorism or the introduction of cryptocurrency. Planet Simple scenario analysis rises to meet this challenge by determining a range of financial effects that climate change may have on a business, with a view to declaring *resilience* on the basis of a relatively insignificant financial effect. These analyses see the determination of a dollar figure (value at risk, percentage change in EBITDA, etc.) as the aim of the exercise. This view of scenario analysis is bolstered by Planet Simple investors, who seek a measurable, discrete financial figure to input into their analyses.

Setting aside the trap of how quantification and false precision can engender spurious certitude (chapter 5), the issue here is that understanding financial effects is the *means* to developing a climate-resilient strategy. Determining potential financial effects—whether quantified or not—is not the ultimate objective of the analysis. The ultimate objective is developing a climate-resilient strategy, and future projections, on their own, "do not tell a decision-maker what to do."[243]

A recent analysis that I reviewed disclosed that the company may experience a 1 percent impact to revenues because of climate-related reputational effects.[244] The analysis said that they made the effort to determine the 1 percent impact even though there were no established methods for doing so, and that the figure is based on expert consensus.[245] Spurious certitude usually isn't this easy to spot. As an informed investor in this business, I would not be sold that the business is resilient because a bunch of people sat around a table and came up with 1 percent impact to revenues. That figure is not what I am interested in, even if it were able to be determined with certainty (which this instance most certainly is not). Instead, I would want to understand the uncertainties and assumptions underpinning the impact and what the company is doing to learn more about these uncertainties and adapt over time. In this way, scenario analysis is more about understanding the uncertainties and assumptions driving financial effects, rather than today's estimate of the potential consequences themselves.

ACTION PLANNING FOR RESILIENCE

Once you have identified your most consequential business impacts, and the climate-related changes and developments that could lead to these impacts under various scenarios, the task turns to integrating these insights into your strategy and business model. We will break this down by integration into corporate risk management and integration into strategic planning.

Integrating into Corporate Risk Management

On Planet Simple, climate risks are itemized as novel, standalone risks separate from other business risks. Many traps of this approach to climate risk have been covered already. Considering climate risks as standalone risks also makes it difficult to integrate them into corporate risk management. In particular, it becomes tempting to assign all of the climate risks to the sustainability team—resulting in an unrealistic burden and inefficient duplication of risk ownership across the organization.

The TCFD pointed out that "in most situations, climate-related risks are drivers of existing risks."[246] Consider the following risks commonly identified in a scenario analysis process:

- The risk of worsening property damage from increased extreme weather impact

- The risk of production stoppages from heatwave-related energy blackouts

- The risk of increased expenses from carbon pricing

- The risk of poor talent attraction and retention at locations with increasing oppressive heat and drought

The sustainability team is not the best risk owner for any of these risks. More suitable owners can be found in property, real estate, business continuity, finance, government relations, and human resource functions. The sustainability team is better placed to ensure that these functions have the right information about future scenarios, so that they can incorporate the insights into their own risk management. For example:

- Sustainability teams can ensure business continuity exercises use forward projections of warming, rather than basing decisions on current state and past experience alone.

- Sustainability teams can offer insight into future carbon pricing possibilities, helping prevent the business from inadvertently making investments that set up future carbon pricing liabilities. Going one step further, sustainability teams can help functions make use of internal carbon pricing to account for emissions-related liabilities.[247]

Integrating into Strategic Planning

When integrating scenario analysis insights into strategic planning, it is important to remember that the exercise is not about optimizing for the most likely scenario (the technical rationality of Planet Simple). Instead, it is about finding a way forward that is robust to the unavoidable uncertainty of making planning and investment decisions on Planet Earth (procedural rationality).

Part of a robust way forward involves investing in what scenario analysis experts refer to as *no regrets* strategies; these authors mention how *no regrets* actions improve on Planet Simple strategies because they make sense regardless of how the future unfolds.[248] In their words, *no regrets* strategies:

> ...make sense economically or in other ways regardless of anthropogenic climate change. The reduction of scientific uncertainty through better predictions and the improvement in the communication of scientific uncertainty are not the only means of reducing net losses and vulnerability. Action on "no regrets"...strategies...are procedurally rational despite profound uncertainties that cannot be eliminated by scientific research.[249]

Examples of *no regrets* actions include:

- Investing in physical risk preparedness, because increases in physical risk are guaranteed for the near term no matter the scenario[250]

- Investing in energy efficiency initiatives that reduce energy use, GHG emissions, and offer long-term value through cost reductions

- Internal activities to plan for scenario triggers (see below) or enhance decision-making and risk management (e.g., internal carbon pricing, employee training on climate-related impacts)

Not every possible action identified in a scenario analysis is a *no regrets* action. Some actions only make good business sense once specific climate-related changes or developments occur. For example, investing in deep decarbonization may only make business sense if a carbon price is actually introduced in a specific location. Making this investment now may be a bad business decision, but a business will need to be ready to move quickly if the carbon price scenario is realized. Making plans for these scenario triggers is known as *conditional strategies* or sometimes just *backup plans*. In addition to devising these backup plans, companies should monitor trigger variables that could change the likelihood of business impacts over time. Example triggers to monitor include:

- The introduction of carbon pricing schemes or carbon border adjustment mechanisms

- Incentives or breakthroughs in low emissions or emissions removal technology

- Policy, reputation, or economic consequences related to deforestation

- Requirements for increased disclosure of climate-related risks, opportunities, and performance metrics

- Signals that the Earth is approaching or passing tipping points that could trigger runaway climate change

ANNUAL RESILIENCE ASSESSMENTS

The purpose of a climate scenario analysis is to identify uncertain, but important, climate-related changes and developments that may affect your strategy (the same logic applies to scenario analysis for any sustainability matter other than climate). If you've identified critical climate-related changes and developments, and have an action plan that can be implemented as these changes and developments unfold, you may be able to claim that your strategy is resilient to climate change.

The climate-related changes and developments in your scenarios, and the action plans that would address them, are based on assumptions of how the future may unfold. This is the procedurally rational way to deal with uncertainty, but it means that the resilience of your strategy is dependent on these assumptions. Ensuring the ongoing resilience of your strategy means revisiting the assumptions as they evolve each year. Revisiting the assumptions does not mean you need to redo the entire scenario analysis—you don't need to identify new climate-related changes or developments or identify new scenario archetypes. Instead, you should review how the world has changed since your scenario analysis and update any underlying assumptions as appropriate.

This is the difference between a *resilience assessment* and a *scenario analysis*. Resilience assessments are completed each year, whereas a scenario analysis only needs to be completed with major changes to strategy or the operating environment.[251]

It's Everyone's Job

As we come to the end of this chapter, it may seem like an overwhelming task to put these practices into place. But if we remember a main premise of this book—that businesses have *always* relied on environmental and social factors to create value—it may become clear that I am advocating for reform of existing practice and not the adoption of something entirely new and additional.

An analogy from decades ago may help clarify further. After a series of scandals and incidents in the 1970s, there was a concerted push to recognize that many issues cut across everyone in the business. Take the issue of safety at work. It is now recognized that safety is part of everyone's job description and not managed by one silo of the organization.

So it is with corporate sustainability. Once we acknowledge the multi-capital model of value creation (chapter 7) and use it to articulate how environmental and social issues affect business success (recall the description of climate-related issues by type of capital earlier in this chapter), it becomes easier to understand how issues like climate change should be part of everyone's job. For example:

- If increasing severity and frequency of extreme weather threaten company property, then facilities/operations teams are best placed to manage it (not the sustainability team)

- If future emissions reduction policies result in government incentives for electric vehicles, then government relations and R&D teams should be across what is happening

In these instances, climate change is owned by relevant functions, with the sustainability team ensuring that the functions have what they need (scenarios of future change, reporting frameworks) and are able to collaborate across functions effectively.

In chapter 2, we discussed the Planet Simple trap of viewing sustainability as separate to core business, and thus relegated to a Public Affairs, Marketing, or Philanthropy function—essentially an obligatory "side dish" or charity effort. As a result, many team members in the business might not think that they are a "sustainability" person. That's someone else's job. Like with safety at work, however, sustainability can no longer be wholly owned and implemented by a sustainability team on its own. It's everyone's job.

Having stepped through how corporate sustainability is fundamental to corporate value creation and explaining how we can integrate it into corporate strategy and governance, we will turn to the final component of managing for resilience on Planet Earth.

CHAPTER 9

Resilience on Planet Earth

> *We need people not to feel they are entering into compliance but entering into genuine value [creation]. And that will come.*
>
> **—Lee White, former managing director, IFRS Foundation**

There is an intriguing duality to corporate reporting today. On the one hand, it is loathed as a compliance *burden* with little strategic value (see chapter 6). On the other hand, very few documents published by a business have as many eyes dedicated to their preparation than an annual report. The attention granted to corporate reports suggests that the loathing may be less about their perceived strategic irrelevance, and more because of the inevitable connection between reporting and evaluation—and therefore accountability.

Our journey from Planet Simple to Planet Earth concludes with reporting not because it is the final task in a linear process, but because it is the component of Planet Simple business most in crisis and most in need of change. Today's financial statements and associated commentary paint a picture of business performance that falls prey to the ultimate trap of Planet Simple (chapter 4). Businesses report on financial results without reference to environmental and social context. The quarterly reporting rhythm assumes that ongoing efficiency gains, quarter-on-quarter, are the objective, giving businesses little latitude to account for inevitable variability in the operating environment. Finally, financial statements facilitate judgments based on outcomes, assuming the outcomes are a linear result of management strategy and action.

The increasing awareness that business value is inextricably linked with environmental and social factors (Planet Earth) has put pressure on companies to articulate a broader picture of performance than the financial statements allow. The vast majority of CEOs say they are too short-term focused and express concerns that quarterly reporting amplifies short-term pressures.[252] Investments that make good business sense over longer time horizons are deprioritized because they may have a negative effect on short-term earnings. Herein lies a central challenge to leaving Planet Simple—if we subscribe to the Planet Simple view that businesses can manage for efficiency and achieve quarterly increases, there is no latitude for them to pivot to the long-term view required for Planet Earth. The result is the ultimate trap of Planet Simple—more short-termism, more attempts to achieve efficiency through control, and a bigger crisis once the variability and unpredictability of Planet Earth makes itself known.

If a paradigm is ripe for revolution when it is in crisis, and the proliferation of alternative frameworks is symbolic of crisis, there is no bigger crisis and revolution underway than in the corporate reporting space. Myriad reporting frameworks, commonly referred to as alphabet soup, have been proposed for painting a broader, more complete picture of business performance. In recent years, however, the alphabet soup has started to congeal, offering a path through the crisis--a path to leave Planet Simple.

From Efficiency to Resilience

In 2022, the IFRS Foundation formed the ISSB to clean up the alphabet soup and develop a global standard for sustainability reporting. Inaugural ISSB Chair Emmanuel Faber stated that because of the scale of global change, "resilience is the new efficiency."[253] When launching the first set of ISSB Standards,[254] Faber described them as a new common language for more resilient businesses.[255]

Faber's emphasis on using language to move from efficiency to resilience is indicative of the paradigm shift needed. According to Kuhn, paradigm shifts change the very language in which we speak about some aspect of the world. The importance of language cannot be understated. It is not some utilitarian tool invented by us after we achieved our current state of human consciousness. In contrast, it is language that makes us human. To quote Fukuyama:

> The emergence of language among early human beings opened up huge new opportunities for both improved coop-eration and cognitive development in an intimately linked fashion… The development of language now only permits the short-term coordination of action but also opens up the possibility of abstraction and theory, critical cognitive faculties that are unique to human beings. Words can refer to concrete objects as well as to abstract classes of objects (dogs, trees) and to abstractions that refer to invisible forces (Zeus, gravity). Putting the two together makes possible mental models—that is general statements about causation.[256]

Reporting can be seen as a mental model of how the business works, and this mental model can only be as rich as the language available to describe it. Too often, language can be limiting. In *The Master and His Emissary*, McGilchrist writes:

> The existence of a system of thought dependent on language automatically devalues whatever cannot be expressed in language; the process of reasoning discounts whatever cannot be reached by reasoning... But in its own terms there is no way that language can break out of the world language creates. Yet it is only whatever can leap beyond the world of language and reason that can break out of the imprisoning hall of mirrors and reconnect us with the lived world.[257]

The ISSB is trying to break out of the conventional language of business because it understands the fundamental mindset shift required to get from efficiency (Planet Simple) to resilience (Planet Earth). The ISSB Standards recognize that business value creation is inextricably linked with society and environment. They recognize that the traditional financial statements are imprisoning business in a short-term focus and a narrow view of the types of *capital* that are important for success. Arguably most important for resilience, however, is how the new standards advocate for a shift to procedural rationality, as we will now consider.

Reporting Is Strategy, Strategy Is Reporting

When asked how long it should take companies to prepare sustainability-related financial disclosure, former IFRS Foundation executive Lee White said the question "can conjure up the sense that this is a compliance exercise and, genuinely, that's not where we need people to be...We need people not to feel they are entering into compliance but entering into genuine value delivery. And that will come."[258]

Imagine asking the question, "How long should it take for companies to evaluate their strategy?" The answer is along the lines of "as long as it needs to take"—no one ever speaks of a *strategy burden*.

In Part II, I explained why the Planet Simple mindset deems reporting to be a compliance exercise with little strategic value (Figure 14).

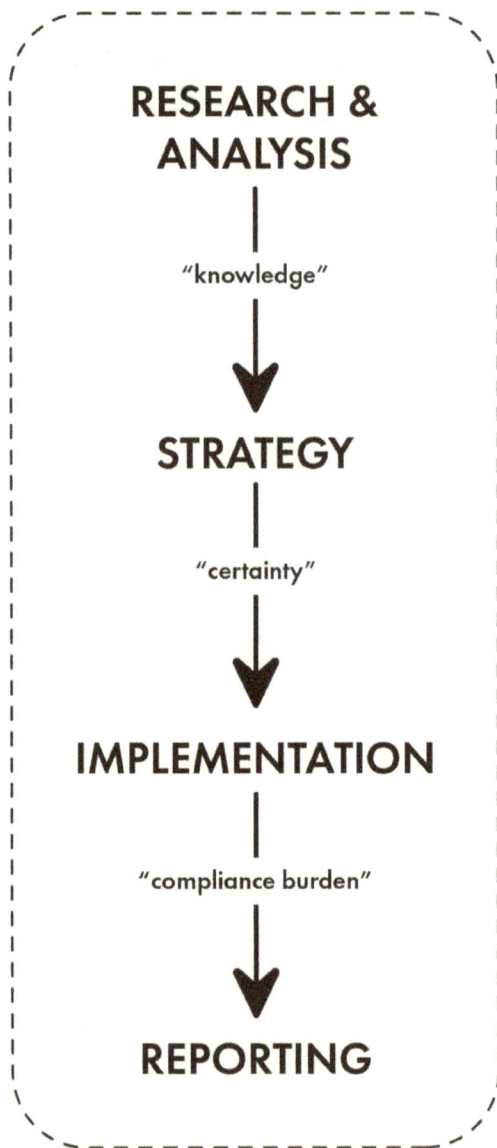

Figure 14. On Planet Simple, reporting is deprioritized as a compliance exercise with little strategic value. This is because Planet Simple prioritizes a top-down, command-and-control decision-making and implementation structure that cannot acknowledge uncertainty in decisions, leaving no room for reporting to support organizational learning.

As I hope this book has made clear, however, we are not on Planet Simple. We are on Planet Earth, where businesses are nested systems in a changing external context, where decisions are never certain, and where strategies seldom proceed in a linear fashion. Given this reality, it may be better to visualize reporting as a crucial tool for understanding performance at the organizational scale, the same scale as strategy development (recall the importance of scale for resilience, as discussed in chapter 4). When we acknowledge uncertainty in strategy, reporting becomes the essential mechanism for generating bottom-up knowledge within a learning organization (recall our discussion of adaptive management in chapter 6; Figure 15).

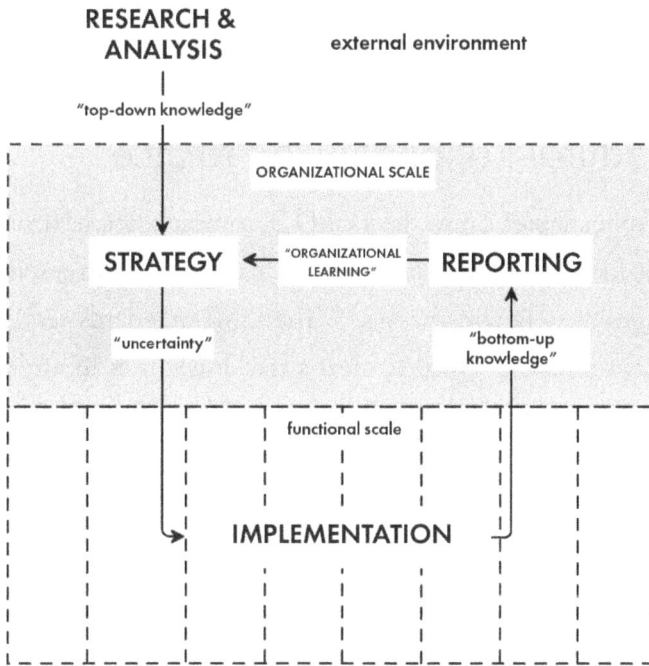

Figure 15. Reporting may be characterized as an organization-wide initiative that generates bottom-up knowledge useful for evolving a corporate strategy over time and supporting ongoing adaptation to change through learning.

This should resonate with you if you've been part of a sustainability reporting process at a company, particularly a process seeking alignment with one of today's comprehensive sustainability reporting standards. Few other processes involve as many contributors across as many functions as a sustainability reporting process, a process lovingly framed as "herding cats" by many. Engaging individuals and teams on their achievements during the year, and their plans for the future, is an immensely valuable knowledge-generating process. In fact, performing a company-wide evaluation, identifying opportunities for improvement, and agreeing on forward ambition look a lot like strategy development. That's why on Planet Earth, reporting is anything but a compliance exercise: *reporting is strategy, and strategy is reporting.*

Procedural Rationality in Practice

Recall from chapter 2 how the TCFD Recommendations (from 2017) were the first to ask business to articulate its *resilience* to sustainability challenges like climate change.[259] The ISSB Standards retained this focus on resilience,[260] which means that businesses in any country adopting the standards will be expected to move from Planet Simple efficiency to Planet Earth resilience. The ESRS say it too.[261]

In addition to advocating for the strategic importance of reporting, today's resilience-focused frameworks (which include the TCFD, ISSB Standards, and ESRS) seek to shift business from the technical rationality of Planet Simple to the procedural rationality of Planet Earth (see chapter 5 for the discussion of technical and procedural rationality). Technical rationality seeks certainty even if it is spurious, and decisions are judged on whether they got the answer right. Procedural rationality embraces uncertainty and judges decisions on whether they followed the right process.

Today's resilience-focused frameworks embrace procedural rationality by emphasizing reporting on *process* in addition to *outcomes*. Unlike financial statements, which are almost exclusively financial metrics, sustainability statements are expected to disclose a company's process for:

- Governance

- Strategy

- Risk Management

- Performance Measurement (metrics and targets)[262]

These four pillars, first introduced by the TCFD Recommendations in 2017, "represent core elements of how organizations operate."[263] By asking for disclosure on how companies manage sustainability-related risks and opportunities through governance, strategy, risk management, and performance measurement, today's frameworks seek information on the process by which companies integrate sustainability into their operations.

By focusing on process, today's resilience-focused reporting frameworks offer untapped strategic value. They can serve as strategic checklists for businesses seeking to integrate sustainability into their operations. The following table offers an example, based on the components of today's resilience-focused frameworks.

Business Component	Strategic Guidance Derived from Reporting Frameworks
Goverance	Integrating sustainability into corporate governance at the board level: • Ensure the board has oversight of material matters • Board oversight of sustainability should be reflected in terms of reference, mandates, role descriptions, and other board-related policies • Ensure a process for determining the board has the appropriate skills and competencies to oversee sustainability matters • Develop a process for informing the board about sustainability matters • Ensure that the board accounts for sustainability matters when overseeing corporate strategy, decisions on major transactions, and risk management • Ensure that the board has oversight of any sustainability-related targets • Consider whether sustainability-related performance metrics should be incorporated into remuneration policies Integrating sustainability into corporate governance at the management level: • Monitoring, managing, and overseeing sustainability matters should be clearly integrated into specific management roles and/or committees • Clear controls and procedures should be specified for sustainability matters, and integrated with other internal functions as appropriate (see chapter 8)
Strategy	Integrating sustainability into strategic planning: • Ensure a clear understanding of how sustainability matters may affect the business model, value chain, and forward prospects • Ensure the consideration of a longer-term time horizon, commensurate with corporate strategic planning process and industry-specific considerations such as the useful life of assets • For sustainability-related opportunities, ensure their consideration is part of strategic planning like any other market opportunity • Obtain agreement on how sustainability matters may affect cash flows today and into the long term • Factor sustainability matters, and their connections to financial performance, into traditional financial planning processes Integrating sustainability into corporate policies: • Policies should relate to one (or more) of the company's material sustainability matters (see chapter 7). • The scope of the policy—in terms of activities, value chain, geographies, stakeholders covered—should be commensurate with the scope of the relevant sustainability matters. • Policies should state the organizational role accountable for its implementation. • Policies should state any relevant legislation or voluntary standards/commitments as applicable. • Affected stakeholders should be involved when developing the policy. • Policies should be made available to affected stakeholders and/or disclosed publicly. Developing sustainability action plans: • Action plans should align with policy objectives and articulate how company investments and actions lead to desired outcomes related to material matters (see chapter 8 discussion on impact logics). • Action plans should align with the scope of relevant sustainability matters and policies, in terms of activities, value chain, geographies, and stakeholders. • Actions should have a clear time horizon, or be designated as ongoing actions. • Action plans should consider trade-offs between sustainability matters—such as a pivot to bio-based input materials that reduces reliance on petroleum extraction but increases pressure on land conversion, or closure of operations that may reduce emissions but increase unemployment. • Action plans should be associated with capex and/or opex planning as appropriate, with any significant sustainability-related expenditures itemized separately to facilitate disclosure on the legitimacy of the action plan.

Business Component	Strategic Guidance Derived from Reporting Frameworks
Risk Management	Integrating sustainability into corporate risk management: • Establish a process to identify, assess, prioritize, and monitor sustainability-related risks. • Risk identification and assessment should make use of reputable information sources. • Risk identification, assessment, and monitoring should consider scenario analysis to explore future uncertainty (see chapter 8). • Establish qualitative (and quantitative, where applicable) frameworks for assessing the severity, magnitude, and likelihood of sustainability risks. • Seek to understand how sustainability risks are drivers of existing corporate risks, before assessing sustainability risks as standalone risks (see chapter 8). • Establish a regular rhythm of sustainability-related risk management, integrated with annual corporate risk management processes.
Performance Measurement (Metrics and Targets)	Defining performance metrics for sustainability: • Adopt performance metrics relevant for material sustainability matters, as defined in global standards (ISSB, GRI) or country-level standards (ESRS). • Ensure internal data collection processes and controls would meet assurance expectations if required. • Ensure metrics are useful for evaluating the effectiveness of policies and action plans for relevant sustainability matters. Defining sustainability-related targets: • Targets should support one or more policy objectives related to sustainability matters. • Targets should have a defined target level or milestone. • Targets should have a clear scope, in terms of whether it applies to business operations and/or value chain, specific geographies, etc. • Targets should have a baseline value and base year against which progress is measured. • Longer-term targets should have defined interim targets or milestones. • Ensure a shared understanding of the assumptions used to define targets. • Define triggers for when a target may need to change in the future (it happens!), and ensure sufficient documentation of the change and its rationale.

On Planet Simple, no one looks to reporting frameworks for strategic guidance. In order to leave Planet Simple, this needs to change because on Planet Earth, *reporting is strategy and strategy is reporting.*

"Seeing" the Future of Corporate Sustainability

The Greek philosopher Empedocles formulated the classical theory of four elements—water, earth, fire, and air—and Aristotle reinforced this idea by characterizing them as moist, dry, hot, and cold. Fire was thus thought of as a substance, and burning was seen as a process of decomposition that applied only to compounds of the elements.

However, the classical theory was thrown into crisis when it was found that burning resulted in a transfer of substance from earthly elements to the air. This led to the development of phlogiston theory, a premise proposed in the late 1600s by Johann Becher, in which flammable materials contained *phlogiston* (a Greek word for "burn") that was released during the combustion process.[264] After something burned, the air around it (which was still seen as simply air) would have more phlogiston as a result of the combustion.

Popularly accepted for some time, the phlogiston theory was thrown into crisis because it was unable to explain why some metals gain weight after they burn. We now know this is because combustion fuses atoms of the metal with oxygen in the air to form a metal oxide. At the time, though, it was all just air and phlogiston.

One of the more longstanding proponents of phlogiston theory was English scientist Joseph Priestly. In 1774, one of his experiments resulted in a gas that burned "five or six times as good as common air."[265] He called this new gas "dephlogisticated air" on the theory that it supported combustion so well because it had no phlogiston in it.[266]

Antoine Lavoisier, another scientific protagonist from that era, came from a different school of thought. He acknowledged that phlogiston theory could not explain why some metals gained weight and was increasingly unable to account for the variety of "airs" that were being discovered. Lavoisier repeated Priestley's experiment and concluded that "common air" is not a single substance. Instead, he called the new gas oxygen—one component of common air—and proposed a theory of combustion that excluded phlogiston.[267]

Looking closer at their respective experiments, Priestley and Lavoisier had the same substance in front of them. They stood before the same exact thing. Priestley saw *dephlogisticated air.* Lavoisier saw *oxygen.*

It is not uncommon for two people to look at the same thing and come to different conclusions about what it actually is. Many of us will look at the figure below and see a vase, until someone else says that they see two silhouettes looking at each other. This *Gestalt switch* is what Kuhn refers to when revolutions in thought cannot occur incrementally. They must happen all at once. Furthermore, once the revolution has occurred, there is no going back.

There are many instances where simplicity is a virtue in navigating our everyday. But there are also times when simplicity can fail us. (As Einstein said, "Make everything as simple as possible, but no simpler."[268]) It is far simpler to suggest that our planet is made up of earth, air, fire, and water, than the hundred or so elements on the periodic table. We know better now, and there is no going back.

It is far simpler to see our planet as S-I-M-P-L-E, than as the messy, complex, and unpredictable reality it actually is. Planet Simple worked for us in biblical times, and for the Enlightenment thinkers who gave us democracy and the scientific method. But it is failing us as a global species, something that we could not have predicted hundreds of years ago. We know better now, and we need to move on.

We started our journey with an introduction to Planet Simple and its dominance. I guided you through how today's global challenges have thrown Planet Simple into crisis and resulted in calls for business to manage for *resilience*. We reviewed the ESG investing boom and how, despite its shortcomings, it is an expected phase that any revolution goes through on its way to widespread adoption.

I gave you a crash course in resilience science and how its real-world observations offer a worldview that *quite simply describes reality better* than Planet Simple. We covered how scenario analysis and adaptive management, examples of decision-making tools that acknowledge uncertainty and change, overcome the shortcomings of Planet Simple decisions—where we succumb to spurious certitude and fail to learn. We concluded with practical guidance on assessing how sustainability affects value creation, integrating sustainability into strategy and governance, and turning reporting from a *burden* into a strategic exercise.

It has been a journey of awareness, which is the precondition for change. Lavoisier *saw* oxygen because his awareness of difficulties with the prevailing theory gave him a sense that something was amiss. He was prepared to *see* oxygen for what it really is.

But along this journey of awareness, I have pointed out Planet Simple traps. Traps that represent what Kuhn would say is the prevailing paradigm trying to fit reality (Planet Earth) into its preexisting box. Like Joseph Priestley when he saw *dephlogisticated air* instead of oxygen, we fall into the Planet Simple traps when we fail to *see* corporate sustainability for what it really is.

It is a recognition that business success has always been inextricably linked with environmental and social context, and a call to transform our mindset to suit. Corporate sustainability is not something new.

It's always been there. Like Lavoisier, we must challenge the prevailing mindset in order to *see* the solution in front of us. The solution is not to leave Planet Earth. Instead, we must leave Planet Simple.

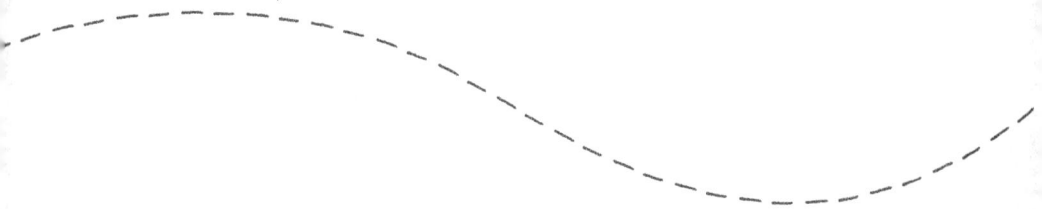

ABOUT THE AUTHOR

Dr. Alex Gold is the CEO of the North America office of BWD Strategic. His team partners with companies large and small as they seek to transform their operations with sustainability at the core.

Born and raised in the US state of Maryland, Dr. Gold graduated from Amherst College with a degree in biology before moving to Sydney, Australia, to pursue a PhD in resilience science at the University of New South Wales. After nearly a decade working with corporate executives and boards in Australia, he returned to the United States on a mission to transform American business so it seizes the tremendous opportunity that sustainability presents.

He has been described as the consummate corporate strategist, making it easy for companies to integrate sustainability through established methods of adaptive governance and resilience thinking. If he's not with the BWD team in New York or Arizona, you'll probably find him in an RV somewhere in between, taking in the wonder of the American landscape.

To connect with Dr. Alex Gold, please scan the QR code below:

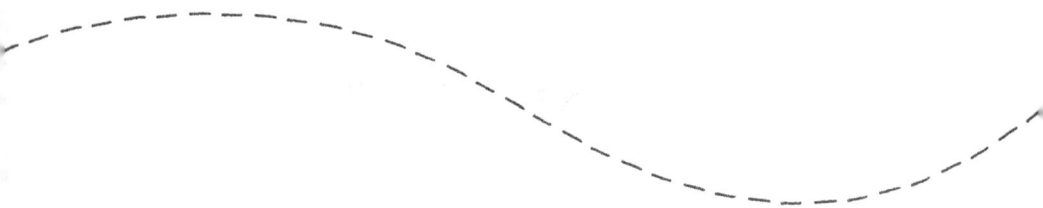

ENDNOTES

1   Margi Murphy, "Flaming Hell: Stephen Hawking says the Earth will become a sizzling fireball by 2600 and humanity will become extinct," The Sun, November 6, 2017, sec. Science.

2   Jane Arraf, "Leave Earth before it's too late, Carl Sagan warns," Tampa Bay Times, December 13, 1994, https://www.tampabay.com/archive/1994/12/13/leave-earth-before-it-s-too-late-carl-sagan-warns/.

3   Elizabeth Weise, "Amazon's Jeff Bezos says we need to leave Earth to survive. First stop: a city on the Moon," USA Today, May 29, 2018, https://www.usatoday.com/story/tech/talkingtech/2018/05/29/amazons-jeff-bezos-says-we-need-leave-earth-survive/651715002/.

4   Thomas Kuhn, *The Structure of Scientific Revolutions: 50th Anniversary Edition*, 4th ed. (Chicago: University of Chicago Press, 2012).

5   Ibid.

6   Ibid., 116.

7   Ibid., 24.

8   Kuhn, *The Structure of Scientific Revolutions: 50th Anniversary Edition*, 71.

9   Holy Bible, New International Version®, NIV® Copyright ©1973, 1978, 1984, 2011, https://www.biblegateway.com/passage/?search=Genesis%201:25-27&version=NIV.

10   John Locke, *Second Treatise of Government*, ed. C. B. Macpherson (Cambridge, MA: Hackett Publishing, 1980).

11   Francis Bacon, *New Atlantis* (London: J. Crooke, 1660).

12   Herbert Butterfield, *The Origins of Modern Science: Revised Edition* (New York: Free Press, 1997).

13   Rene Descartes, *Discourse on Method and Meditations on First Philosophy*, 4th ed. (Indianapolis: Hackett Publishing Company, 2006).

14   Francis Fukuyama, *Liberalism and its Discontents*, (New York; Farrar, Straus, and Giroux; 2022), 85.

15   Thomas Hobbes and Crawford B. Macpherson, *Leviathan*, Repr, Penguin Classics (Harmondsworth: Penguin Books, 1988).

16   Francis Fukuyama, *Political Order and Political Decay: From the Industrial Revolution to the Globalization of Democracy* (New York: Farrar, Straus and Giroux, 2015).

17   Fukuyama, *Liberalism and its Discontents*.

18   Fukuyama, *Political Order and Political Decay: From the Industrial Revolution to the Globalization of Democracy*

19   Adam Smith, *The Wealth of Nations* (Middletown, DE: Shine Classics, 2014).

20   Milton Friedman, "A Friedman Doctrine - the social responsibility of business is to increase its profits," The New York Times, September 13, 1970, https://www.nytimes.com/1970/09/13/archives/a-friedman-doctrine-the-social-responsibility-of-business-is-to.html.

21 Margaret Thatcher, "Interview for 'Woman's Own' ('No Such Thing as Society')," in *Margaret Thatcher Foundation: Speeches, Interviews and Other Statements* (London, 1987).

22 Ibid.

23 Joshua Farley and Megan Egler, "Panarchy and the Economy," in *Applied Panarchy: Applications and Diffusion across Disciplines*, ed. Lance H. Gunderson, Craig Reece Allen, and Ahjond Garmestani (Washington, DC: Island Press, 2022).

24 Nicholas Hassim Taleb, *The Black Swan: The Impact of the Highly Improbable* (New York: Random House, 2007).

25 Ibid.

26 Nassim N. Taleb, *The Black Swan: The Impact of the Highly Improbable*.

27 Ibid.

28 Daniel Kahneman, *Thinking, Fast and Slow* (New York: Farrar, Straus and Giroux, 2011).

29 Cited in Donald Rapp, *Bubbles, Booms, and Busts: The Rise and Fall of Financial Assets* (New York: Copernicus Books, 2009), 34.

30 Kahneman, *Thinking, Fast and Slow*, 87.

31 Ibid., 201.

32 Frederick Winslow Taylor, *The Principles of Scientific Management* (Mineola: Dover Publications, 1998).

33 Matthew Stewart, *The Management Myth: Debunking Modern Business Philosophy* (New York, London: W. W. Norton, 2010).

34 J. A. Merkle, "Scientific Management," in *International Encyclopedia of Public Policy and Administration*, ed. J. M. Shafritz (Boulder: Westview Press, 1998), 2036–2040.

35 Nancy K. Sandars, *The Epic of Gilgamesh: An English Version, with an Introduction* (New York: Penguin, 1972).

36 John Perlin, *A Forest Journey: The Role of Wood in the Development of Civilization* (Cambridge: Harvard University Press, 1991).

37 Isaac Deutcher, *The Prophet Unarmed: Trotsky:* 1921-1929 (Oxford, Oxford University Press, 1954).

38 Library of Congress, "George Perkins Marsh," n.d., sec. Today in History - September 30, https://www.loc.gov/item/today-in-history/september-30/.

39 Upton Sinclair, *The Jungle: The Uncensored Original Edition* (Tucson: Sharp Press, 1905).

40 "Upton Sinclair", Social History (biography), archived from the original (blog) on May 27, 2012.

41 Ibid., 29.

42 Carson, Rachel, *Silent Spring* (Boston: Houghton Mifflin, 2002).

43 Dorothy McLaughlin, "Fooling with nature: *Silent Spring* revisited," Frontline, PBS. Archived from the original on March 10, 2010.

44 Mark Hamilton Lytle, *The Gentle Subversive: Rachel Carson, Silent Spring, and the Rise of the Environmental Movement* (New York: Oxford University Press, 2007) 166–167.

45 Brian M. Thomsen, *The Dream That Will Not Die: Inspiring Words of John, Robert, and Edward Kennedy* (New York: Macmillan, 2010) 126–127.

46　Friedman, "A Friedman Doctrine—the social responsibility of business is to increase its profits."

47　Eunice Foote, "Circumstances Affecting the Heat of Sun's Rays," American Journal of Art and Science, 2nd Series, v. XXII/no. LXVI (November 1856): 382–383.

48　John Perlin, "Science Knows No Gender? In Search of Eunice Foote, Who, 162 Years Ago Discovered the Principal Cause of Global Warming." Speech delivered May 17, 2018 at the University of California – Santa Barbara.

49　Lance H Gunderson, Craig R. Allen, and Ahjond S. Garmestani, "Applications and Diffusion of Panarchy Theory," in *Applied Panarchy: Applications and Diffusion across Disciplines*, ed. Lance H. Gunderson, Craig Reece Allen, and Ahjond Garmestani (Washington, DC: Island Press, 2022), 293.

50　In this sense, the natural environment is considered a "silent" stakeholder.

51　Bill McNabb, Ram Charan, and Dennis C. Carey, *Talent, Strategy, Risk: How Investors and Boards Are Redefining TSR* (Boston: Harvard Business Review Press, 2021), 5.

52　World Economic Forum, "The universal purpose of a company in the fourth industrial revolution," (Davos, 2019), 1, https://www3.weforum.org/docs/WEF_AM20_Davos_Manifesto.pdf.

53　Kuhn, *The Structure of Scientific Revolutions: 50th Anniversary Edition*, 24.

54　United Nations Global Compact, International Finance Corporation, and Swiss Federal Department of Foreign Affairs, "Who cares wins: connecting financial markets to a changing world," 2005, https://www.unepfi.org/fileadmin/events/2004/stocks/who_cares_wins_global_compact_2004.pdf.

55   Robert G. Eccles, Ioannis Ioannou, and George Serafeim, "The Impact of Corporate Sustainability on Organizational Processes and Performance," *Management Science* 60, no. 11 (November 2014): 2835–2857, https://doi.org/10.1287/mnsc.2014.1984.

56   Ibid., 1.

57   Larry Fink, "A sense of purpose," 2018, https://corpgov.law.harvard.edu/2018/01/17/a-sense-of-purpose/.

58   Tariq Fancy, "The secret diary of a sustainable investor," 2021, https://medium.com/@sosofancy/the-secret-diary-of-a-sustainable-investor-part-1-70b6987fa139.

59   Tariq Fancy, "The secret diary of a 'sustainable investor' - Part 4 (Epilogue)," 2022, https://medium.com/@sosofancy/the-secret-diary-of-a-sustainable-investor-part-4-epilogue-f18304fd9db7.

60   Fancy, "The secret diary of a sustainable investor."

61   Ibid.

62   Ibid

63   Fancy, "The secret diary of a sustainable investor."

64   Ibid.

65   DWS, "2020 annual report," March 2021. vi.

66   Patricia Kowsmann and Ken Brown, "Fired executive says Deutsche Bank's DWS overstated sustainable-investing efforts," Wall Street Journal, August 1, 2021, sec. Markets, https://www.wsj.com/articles/fired-executive-says-deutsche-banks-dws-overstated-sustainable-investing-efforts-11627810380.

67   Ibid.

68   Ibid.

69   Ibid.

70   Ibid.

71   James Mackintosh, "Why the sustainable investment craze is flawed," The Wall Street Journal, January 23, 2022, sec. Finance, https://www.wsj.com/articles/why-the-sustainable-investment-craze-is-flawed-11642865789.

72   Ibid.

73   Ibid.

74   Derek Brower, Amanda Chu, and Myles McCormick, "The energy transition will be volatile," Financial Times, June 29, 2023, sec. Markets, https://www.ft.com/content/86d71297-3f34-48f3-8f3f-28b7e8be03c6.

75   Gartner, "Gartner hype cycle," 2024, https://www.gartner.com/en/research/methodologies/gartner-hype-cycle.

76   Ibid.

77   C. S. Holling, "Resilience and Stability of Ecological Systems," *Annual Review of Ecology and Systematics* 4 (1973): 1–23.

78   Fikret Berkes and Carl Folke, eds., *Linking Social and Ecological Systems: Management Practices and Social Mechanisms for Building Resilience* (Cambridge: Cambridge University Press, 1998); C. Folke, "Resilience: The Emergence of a Perspective for Social-Ecological Systems Analyses," *Global Environmental Change* 16, no. 3 (2006): 253–267; G. C. Gallopín, "Linkages between Vulnerability, Resilience, and Adaptive Capacity," *Global Environmental Change* 16, no. 3 (2006): 293–303, https://doi.org/10.1016/j.gloenvcha.2006.02.004; Resilience Alliance, *Assessing and Managing Resilience in Social-Ecological Systems: A Practitioners Workbook. Version 1.0 June 2007* (Stockholm: Resilience Alliance, 2007); Resilience Alliance, *Assessing Resilience in*

Social-Ecological Systems: Workbook for Practitioners. Revised Version 2.0 (Stockholm: Resilience Alliance, 2010), http://www.resalliance.org/srv/file.php/261; Joern Fischer, Garry D. Peterson, Toby A. Gardner, Line J. Gordon, Ioan Fazey, Thomas Elmqvist, Adam Felton, Carl Folke, Stephen Dovers, "Integrating Resilience Thinking and Optimisation for Conservation," *Trends in Ecology & Evolution* 24, no. 10 (2009): 549–554, https://doi.org/10.1016/j.tree.2009.03.020.

79   Francis Westley, Stephen R. Carpenter, William A. Brock, C. S. Holling, Lance H. Gunderson, "Why Systems of People and Nature Are Not Just Social and Ecological Systems," in *Panarchy: Understanding Transformations in Human and Natural Systems*, ed. Lance H. Gunderson and C. S. Holling (Washington: Island Press, 2002), 103–120.

80   Folke, "Resilience: The Emergence of a Perspective for Social-Ecological Systems Analyses."

81   Robin Kundis Craig, B. Cosens, A. Garmestani, and J. Ruhl, "Panarchy and Law in the Anthropocene," in *Applied Panarchy: Applications and Diffusion across Disciplines,* ed. Lance H. Gunderson, Craig Reece Allen, Ahjond Garmestani (Washington: Island Press, 2022).

82   The use of "complexity" here relates to complex adaptive systems. In this usage, complex has a specific meaning and is differentiated from something that is complicated. Complex adaptive systems contain nonlinear relationships between components that vary over space and time, feature variety and novelty constantly being added to the system, and have emergent properties. Emergent properties are those that emerge from unique interactions between components at lower scales, and emergence cannot be predicted from the analysis of component parts. Complex adaptive systems may be contrasted with complicated systems, such as the mechanism of tiny, intricate cogs and springs that drive old-style clocks. Here, the individual pieces are not independent of one another; rather, the movement of one depends on another in an unvarying way and the components do not change over time. Analogy from Brian Walker and David Salt, Resilience Practice:

Building Capacity to Absorb Disturbance and Maintain Function (Washington: Island Press, 2012). "Change is the only constant" is widely attributed to Heraclitus (circa fifth century BCE).

83   C. S. Holling, *Adaptive Environmental Assessment and Management* (London: Wiley, 1978).

84   Daniel Kahneman, *Thinking, Fast and Slow* (New York: Farrar, Straus and Giroux, 2011), 205.

85   Holling, Gunderson, and Ludwig point out that Nature Balanced is the worldview of several organizations with a mandate for reforming global resource and environmental policy, including the Brundtland Commission, the World Resources Institute, the International Institute of Applied Systems Analysis, and the International Institute for Sustainable Development. C. S. Holling, L. H. Gunderson, and Donald Ludwig, "In Quest of a Theory of Adaptive Change," in *Panarchy: Understanding Transformations in Human and Natural Systems,* ed. Lance H. Gunderson and C. S. Holling (Washington: Island Press, 2002), 3–24.

86   Brian Walker and colleagues point out that because of continuous disturbances, human actions, and other changes, it is more appropriate to think about a system as continuously moving about within a particular basin rather than tending directly toward an attractor. Brain Walker, C. S. Holling, Stephen R. Carpenter, and Ann Kinzig, "Resilience, Adaptability and Transformability in Social–Ecological Systems," *Ecology and Society* 9, no. 2 (2004): 5.

87   Lance H. Gunderson, "Ecological Resilience–in Theory and Application," *Annual Review of Ecology and Systematics* 31 (2000): 425–439.

88   For a review see Folke, "Resilience: The Emergence of a Perspective for Social-Ecological Systems Analyses."

89   C. S. Holling, "The Resilience of Terrestrial Ecosystems: Local Surprise and Global Change," in *Sustainable Development of the Biosphere,* ed.

W. C. Clark and R. E. Munn (Cambridge: Cambridge University Press, 1986), 292–317; Lance H. Gunderson, C. S. Holling, and Stephen S. Light, "Barriers Broken and Bridges Built: A Synthesis," in *Barriers and Bridges to the Renewal of Ecosystems and Institutions*, ed. Lance H. Gunderson, C. S. Holling, and Stephen S. Light (New York: Columbia University Press, 1995), 489–532; Gallopín, "Linkages between Vulnerability, Resilience, and Adaptive Capacity."

90   Lance Gunderson, C. S. Holling, and Garry D. Peterson, "Surprises and Sustainability: Cycles of Renewal in the Everglades," in *Panarchy: Understanding Transformations in Human and Natural Systems*, ed. C. S. Holling and Lance H. Gunderson (Washington DC: Island Press, 2002).

91   The worldview that I am introducing as Nature Varied is referred to as Nature Resilient in *Panarchy*.

92   Marten Scheffer, Steve Carpenter, Jonathan A. Foley, Carl Folke & Brian Walker, "Catastrophic Shifts in Ecosystems," *Nature* 413, no. 6856 (2001): 591, https://doi.org/10.1038/35098000.

93   Carl Folke, Steve Carpenter, Brian Walker, Marten Scheffer, Thomas Elmqvist, Lance Gunderson, and C.S. Holling, "Regime Shifts, Resilience, and Biodiversity in Ecosystem Management," *Annual Review of Ecology, Evolution, and Systematics* 35 (2004): 557–581.

94   Gunderson, "Ecological Resilience–in Theory and Application"; Folke et al., "Regime Shifts, Resilience, and Biodiversity in Ecosystem Management."

95   Ann P. Kinzig, Paul Ryan, Michel Etienne, Helen Allison, Thomas Elmqvist, and Brian H. Walker, "Resilience and Regime Shifts: Assessing Cascading Effects," *Ecology and Society* 11, no. 1 (2006): 20.

96   Will Steffen, Johan Rockström, Katherine Richardson, Timothy M. Lenton, Carl Folke, Diana Liverman, Colin P. Summerhayes, Anthony D. Barnosky, Sarah E. Cornell, Michel Crucifix, Jonathan F. Donges,

Ingo Fetzer, Steven J. Lade, Marten Scheffer, Ricarda Winkelmann, and Hans Joachim Schellnhuber, "Trajectories of the Earth System in the Anthropocene," *Proceedings of the National Academy of Sciences* 115, no. 33 (August 14, 2018): 8252–8259, https://doi.org/10.1073/pnas.1810141115.

97   Holling, Gunderson, and Ludwig, "In Quest of a Theory of Adaptive Change."

98   C. S. Holling, "What Barriers? What Bridges?," in *Barriers and Bridges to the Renewal of Ecosystems and Institutions,* ed. Lance H. Gunderson, C. S. Holling, and Stephen S. Light (New York: Columbia University Press, 1995), 3–36.

99   Put another way, an obvious way a system may find itself close to a threshold is because changes to the system itself push it toward a threshold. A less appreciated way a system may find itself on the precipice of a regime shift, however, is because the *threshold has moved closer to the system* because of changes to the shapes of the basins (stability landscape).

100   The adaptive cycle was formalized as a model of ecosystem change by Lance Gunderson and colleagues in their 1995 book *Barriers and Bridges to the Renewal of Ecosystems and Institutions.* It was extended to include social systems in order to serve as a heuristic for understanding social-ecological change in Gunderson and Holling's 2002 seminal work *Panarchy: Understanding Transformations in Human and Natural Systems.* Gunderson, Craig Allen, and Ahjond Garmestani describe how the adaptive cycle has influenced policy, economy, and society more broadly in their 2022 book *Applied Panarchy: Applications and Diffusion across Disciplines.*

101   Brian H. Walker, "Is Succession a Viable Concept in African Savanna Ecosystems?," in *Forest Succession: Concepts and Application*, ed. Darrell C. West, Herman H. Shugart, and Daniel B. Botkin (New York: Springer-Verlag, 1981), 431–447; Holling, "The Resilience of Terres-

trial Ecosystems: Local Surprise and Global Change"; Holling, "What Barriers? What Bridges?"; Lance H. Gunderson and C. S. Holling, eds., *Panarchy: Understanding Transformations in Human and Natural Systems* (Washington: Island Press, 2002).

102 The ultimate trap of Planet Simple is an adaptation of the pathology of natural resource management described by resilience scientists, beginning with Holling and Gary Meffe in 1996. C. S. Holling and Gary K. Meffe, "Command and Control and the Pathology of Natural Resource Management," Conservation Biology 10, no. 2 (1996): 328–337, https://doi.org/10.1016/j.jep.2006.06.016.

103 Brian Walker, Lance Gunderson, Ann Kinzig, Carl Folke, Steve Carpenter, and Lisen Schultz, "A Handful of Heuristics and Some Propositions for Understanding Resilience in Social-Ecological Systems," *Ecology and Society* 11, no. 1 (2006): 13.

104 Joseph Alois Schumpeter, *Capitalism, Socialism, and Democracy* (New York: Harper & Row, 1950).

105 C. S. Holling, "Understanding the Complexity of Economic, Ecological, and Social Systems," *Ecosystems* 4, no. 5 (2001): 390–405.

106 From a biophysical perspective, the structure emerges as the most efficient way to break down, consume, and transfer energy flows within the system. E. D. Schneider and J. J. Kay, "Life as a Manifestation of the Second Law of Thermodynamics," *Mathematical and Computer Modelling* 19, no. 6–8 (March 1994): 25–48, https://doi.org/10.1016/0895-7177(94)90188-0.

107 Ahjond S. Garmestani and Melinda Harm Benson, "A Framework for Resilience-Based Governance of Social-Ecological Systems," *Ecology and Society* 18, no. 1 (2013): art9, https://doi.org/10.5751/ES-05180-180109; Olivia Odom Green, Ahjond S. Garmestani, Craig R. Allen, Lance H. Gunderson, J. B. Ruhl, Craig A. Arnold, Nicholas A. J. Graham, Barbara Cosens, David G. Angeler, Brian C. Chaffin, and C. S. Holling, "Barriers and Bridges to the Integration of Social–Ecologi-

cal Resilience and Law," *Frontiers in Ecology and the Environment* 13, no. 6 (August 2015): 332–37, https://doi.org/10.1890/140294.

108 Garry Peterson, Craig R. Allen, and C. S. Holling, "Ecological Resilience, Biodiversity, and Scale," *Ecosystems* 1 (1998): 6–18.

109 Gunderson, Holling, and Peterson, "Surprises and Sustainability: Cycles of Renewal in the Everglades."

110 Gunderson and Holling, *Panarchy: Understanding Transformations in Human and Natural Systems.*

111 "President passes through flagstaff," The Coconino Sun, May 9, 1903.

112 Peterson, Allen, and Holling, "Ecological Resilience, Biodiversity, and Scale"; W. Neil Adger, Nigel W. Arnell, and Emma L. Tompkins, "Successful Adaptation to Climate Change across Scales," *Global Environmental Change* 15, no. 2 (2005): 77–86, https://doi.org/10.1016/j.gloenvcha.2004.12.005; Walker et al., "A Handful of Heuristics and Some Propositions for Understanding Resilience in Social-Ecological Systems."

113 Folke, "Resilience: The Emergence of a Perspective for Social-Ecological Systems Analyses," 259.

114 Lance H. Gunderson, C. S. Holling, and Stephen S. Light, eds., *Barriers and Bridges to the Renewal of Ecosystems and Institutions* (New York: Columbia University Press, 1995); Gunderson and Holling, *Panarchy: Understanding Transformations in Human and Natural Systems*; Barbara Cosens and Lance Gunderson, eds., *Practical Panarchy for Adaptive Water Governance* (Cham: Springer International Publishing, 2018), https://doi.org/10.1007/978-3-319-72472-0.

115 S. L. Pimm, *The Balance of Nature?* (Chicago: Chicago University Press, 1991); Michael G. Neubert and Hal Caswell, "Alternatives to Resilience for Measuring the Responses of Ecological Systems to Perturbations," *Ecology* 78, no. 3 (1997): 653–65, https://doi.org/10.1890/0012-

9658(1997)078[0653:ATRFMT]2.0.CO;2; Gunderson, "Ecological Resilience–in Theory and Application"; Folke, "Resilience: The Emergence of a Perspective for Social-Ecological Systems Analyses"; Gallopín, "Linkages between Vulnerability, Resilience, and Adaptive Capacity."

116 Holling makes a distinction between engineering resilience and ecological resilience. My use of evolutionary resilience is the same as Holling's ecological resilience. The use of evolutionary is meant to align the worldview with Nature Evolving and align with the aim of supporting a business's evolution in the face of change. C. S. Holling, "Engineering Resilience versus Ecological Resilience," in *Engineering Within Ecological Constraints*, ed. P. Schulze (Washington: National Academy Press, 1996), 31–44.

117 Gunderson, "Ecological Resilience–in Theory and Application," 429.

118 Folke, "Resilience: The Emergence of a Perspective for Social-Ecological Systems Analyses," 259.

119 Walker et al., "A Handful of Heuristics and Some Propositions for Understanding Resilience in Social-Ecological Systems," 259.

120 Ibid., 253.

121 Iain McGilchrist, *The Master and His Emissary: The Divided Brain and the Making of the Western World*, 2nd ed. (Yale University Press, 2019), 232.

122 Joshua Farley and Megan Egler, "Panarchy and the Economy," in *Applied Panarchy: Applications and Diffusion across Disciplines*, ed. Lance H. Gunderson, Craig Reece Allen, and Ahjond Garmestani (Washington, DC: Island Press, 2022), 205.

123 Lance H Gunderson, Craig R. Allen, and Ahjond S. Garmestani, "Applications and Diffusion of Panarchy Theory," in *Applied Panarchy: Applications and Diffusion across Disciplines*, ed. Lance H. Gunderson,

Craig Reece Allen, and Ahjond Garmestani (Washington: Island Press, 2022), 306.

124 I am grateful to Michael Smithson for these metaphors of uncertainty. Michael Smithson, "The Many Faces and Masks of Uncertainty," in *Uncertainty and Risk: Multidisciplinary Perspectives*, ed. Gabrielle Bammer and Michael Smithson (London: Earthscan, 2008), 13–26.

125 Martine Girod-Séville and Véronique Perret, "Epistemological Foundations," in *Doing Management Research: A Comprehensive Guide*, ed. Raymond-Alain Thietart (London: Sage, 2001), 13.

126 Isaiah Berlin, *The Roots of Romanticism* (Princeton University Press, 2001).

127 Ibid.

128 Iain McGilchrist, *The Master and His Emissary: The Divided Brain and the Making of the Western World*, 2nd ed. (Yale University Press, 2019), 426.

129 Horst W. J. Rittel and Melvin M. Webber, "Dilemmas in a General Theory of Planning," *Policy Sciences* 4 (1973): 173.

130 L. Gunderson, "Resilience, Flexibility and Adaptive Management – Antidotes for Spurious Certitude?," *Conservation Ecology* 3 (1999): 7.

131 David Harvey, *The Condition of Postmodernity: An Enquiry into the Origins of Cultural Change* (Oxford: Blackwell, 1990).

132 Ronald D. Brunner and Amanda H. Lynch, *Adaptive Governance and Climate Change* (Boston: American Meteorological Society, 2010), 87.

133 Herman A. Karl, Lawrence E. Susskind, and Katherine H. Wallace, "A Dialogue, Not a Diatribe: Effective Integration of Science and Policy through Joint Fact Finding," *Environment* 49 (2007): 22.

134 Ronald Brunner and Toddi A. Steelman, "Beyond Scientific Management," in *Adaptive Governance: Integrating Science, Policy, and Decision-Making*, ed. Ronald D. Brunner, Toddi A. Steelman, Lindy Coe-Juell, Christina M. Cromley, Christine M. Edwards, and Donna W. Tucker (New York: Columbia University Press, 2005), 1–46; Karl, Susskind, and Wallace, "A Dialogue, Not a Diatribe: Effective Integration of Science and Policy through Joint Fact Finding"; John H. Lawton, "Ecology, Politics, and Policy," *Journal of Applied Ecology* 44 (2007): 465–74; William Ascher, Toddi A. Steelman, and Robert Healy, *Knowledge and Environmental Policy: Re-Imagining the Boundaries of Science and Politics* (Cambridge: The MIT Press, 2010); Brunner and Lynch, *Adaptive Governance and Climate Change*.

135 Ascher, Steelman, and Healy, *Knowledge and Environmental Policy: Re-Imagining the Boundaries of Science and Politics*, 63.

136 Roger A. Pielke, Daniel Sarewitz, and Radford Byerly Jr., "Decision Making and the Future of Nature: Understanding and Using Predictions," in *Prediction: Science, Decision Making, and the Future of Nature*, ed. Daniel Sarewitz, Roger A. Pielke Jr., and Radford Byerly Jr. (Washington: Island Press, 2000), 385.

137 Mark Charlesworth and Chukwumerije Okereke, "Policy Responses to Rapid Climate Change: An Epistemological Critique of Dominant Approaches," *Global Environmental Change* 20, no. 1 (2010): 122, https://doi.org/10.1016/j.gloenvcha.2009.09.001.

138 Daniel Sarewitz, "Science and Environmental Policy: An Excess of Objectivity," in *The Earth Sciences, Philosophy, and the Claims of Community*, ed. R. Frodeman (Upper Saddle River: Prentice Hall, 2000), 79–98, http://www.cspo.org/_old_ourlibrary/ScienceandEnvironmentalPolicy.htm.

139 Brunner and Lynch, *Adaptive Governance and Climate Change*.

140 The concept of something such as climate models having to rely on known data is borrowed from McGilchrist in *The Master and His*

Emissary, when he discusses how the reductionist left hemisphere of the human brain processes information: "Because the left hemisphere is dealing with things that are known, they have to have a degree of fixity: if their constantly changing nature is respected, they cannot be known" (p. 343).

141 Orrin H. Pilkey and Linda Pilkey-Jarvis, *Useless Arithmetic: Why Environmental Scientists Can't Predict the Future* (New York: Columbia University Press, 2007), 184.

142 Ascher, Steelman, and Healy, *Knowledge and Environmental Policy: Re-Imagining the Boundaries of Science and Politics*; Pilkey and Pilkey-Jarvis, *Useless Arithmetic: Why Environmental Scientists Can't Predict the Future.*

143 Wlliam Ascher, "The Ambiguous Nature of Forecasts in Project Evaluation: Diagnosing the over-Optimism of Rate-of-Return Analysis," *International Journal of Forecasting* 9, no. 1 (1993): 109–115; Ascher, Steelman, and Healy, *Knowledge and Environmental Policy: Re-Imagining the Boundaries of Science and Politics.*

144 Nassim N. Taleb, *The Black Swan: The Impact of the Highly Improbable* (New York: Random House, 2007), 61.

145 Sheila Jasanoff, "Technologies of Humility: Citizen Participation in Governing Science," *Minerva* 41, no. 3 (2003): 223–44.

146 Kees van der Heijden, *Scenarios: The Art of Strategic Conversation* (West Sussex: Wiley, 2005).

147 J. H. Chesshire and A. J. Surrey, "World Energy Resources and the Limitations of Computer Modelling," *Long Range Planning* 8, no. 3 (1975): 54–61; Pilkey and Pilkey-Jarvis, *Useless Arithmetic: Why Environmental Scientists Can't Predict the Future*; Audrey Coreau, Gilles Pinay, John D Thompson, Pierre-Olivier Cheptou, and Laurent Mermet, "The Rise of Research on Futures in Ecology: Rebalancing Scenarios and Predictions," *Ecology Letters* 12, no. 12 (2009): 1277–1286, https://doi.org/10.1111/j.1461-0248.2009.01392.x;

Steve Bankes, "Exploratory Modeling for Policy Analysis," *Operations Research* 41, no. 3 (1993): 435–49; Alan Irwin and Brian Wynne, eds., *Misunderstanding Science? The Public Reconstruction of Science and Technology* (Cambridge: Cambridge University Press, 1996); Jasanoff, "Technologies of Humility: Citizen Participation in Governing Science."

148 Ascher, Steelman, and Healy, Knowledge and Environmental Policy: Re-Imagining the Boundaries of Science and Politics, 9–88.

149 Ibid.

150 Ibid.

151 Pilkey and Pilkey-Jarvis, *Useless Arithmetic: Why Environmental Scientists Can't Predict the Future*, 189.

152 Ascher, Steelman, and Healy, *Knowledge and Environmental Policy: Re-Imagining the Boundaries of Science and Politics.*

153 Kahneman, *Thinking, Fast and Slow*, 263.

154 John Bridger Robinson, "Backing into the Future: On the Methodological and Institutional Biases Embedded in Energy Supply and Demand Forecasting," *Technological Forecasting and Social Change* 21, no. 3 (1982): 237.

155 B. L. Turner, Roger E. Kasperson, Pamela A. Matson, James J. McCarthy, Robert W. Corell, Lindsey Christensen, Noelle Eckley, Jeanne X. Kasperson, Amy Luers, Marybeth L. Martello, Colin Polsky, Alexander Pulsipher, and Andrew Schiller, "A Framework for Vulnerability Analysis in Sustainability Science," *Proceedings of the National Academy of Sciences of the United States of America* 100, no. 14 (July 8, 2003): 8074–79, https://doi.org/10.1073/pnas.1231335100.

156 Pielke, Sarewitz, and Byerly Jr., "Decision Making and the Future of Nature: Understanding and Using Predictions."

157 K. O'Brien, Siri Hallstrom Eriksen, Lynn Nygaard, and Ane Schjolden, "Why Different Interpretations of Vulnerability Matter in Climate Change Discourses," *Climate Policy* 7, no. 1 (2007): 80.

158 Timothy D. Mitchell and Mike Hulme, "Predicting Regional Climate Change: Living with Uncertainty," *Progress in Physical Geography* 23 (1999): 57–78; Robert J. Lempert, Michael E. Schlesinger, Steven C. Bankes, and Natalia G. Andronova, "The Impacts of Climate Variability on Near-Term Policy Choices and the Value of Information," *Climatic Change* 45 (2000): 129–61.

159 James D. Ford et al., "Case Study and Analogue Methodologies in Climate Change Vulnerability Research," *Wiley Interdisciplinary Reviews: Climate Change 1*, no. 3 (2010): 381, https://doi.org/10.1002/wcc.48.

160 T. R. Carter, M. L. Parry, H. Harasawa, and S. Nishioka, *IPCC Technical Guidelines for Assessing Climate Change Impacts and Adaptations* (London: University College London, 1994), 11, https://www.ipcc.ch/report/ipcc-technical-guidelines-for-assessing-climate-change-impacts-and-adaptations-2/.

161 Richard Klein, Siri E. H. Eriksen, Lars Otto Næss, Anne Hammill, Thomas M. Tanner, Carmenza Robledo, and Karen L. O'Brien, "Portfolio Screening to Support the Mainstreaming of Adaptation to Climate Change into Development Assistance," *Climatic Change* 84 (2007): 23–44; S. Dovers, "Normalizing Adaptation," *Global Environmental Change* 19, no. 1 (2009): 4–6, https://doi.org/10.1016/j.gloenvcha.2008.06.006; Ford et al., "Case Study and Analogue Methodologies in Climate Change Vulnerability Research."

162 Ford et al., "Case Study and Analogue Methodologies in Climate Change Vulnerability Research," 376.

163 McGilchrist, *The Master and His Emissary: The Divided Brain and the Making of the Western World*, 353.

164 Herbert A. Simon, *The Sciences of the Artificial* (Cambridge: MIT Press, 1996), 25.

165 McGilchrist, *The Master and His Emissary: The Divided Brain and the Making of the Western World*, 437.

166 Vannevar Bush, *Science, the Endless Frontier* (Washington: National Science Foundation, 1960), http://www.nsf.gov/od/lpa/nsf50/vbush1945.htm; Sarewitz, "Science and Environmental Policy: An Excess of Objectivity"; Roger A. Pielke Jr., "When Scientists Politicize Science: Making Sense of Controversy over The Skeptical Environmentalist," *Environmental Science & Policy* 7, no. 5 (2004): 405–417, https://doi.org/10.1016/j.envsci.2004.06.004; Lawton, "Ecology, Politics, and Policy"; M. Hulme, R. Pielke, and S. Dessai, "Keeping Prediction in Perspective," *Nature Reports Climate Change* 3 (2009): 126–127, https://doi.org/10.1038/climate.2009.110; Ascher, Steelman, and Healy, *Knowledge and Environmental Policy: Re-Imagining the Boundaries of Science and Politics*.

167 Radford Jr. Byerly, "Prepared Statement of Radford Byerly, Jr.," in New Directions for Climate Research and Technology Initiatives. Hearing before the Committee on Science, House of Representatives, 107th Congress, 2nd Session, 17 April 2002 (Washington: Government Printing Office, 2002), 40–51, http://commdocs.house.gov/committees/science/hsy78957.000/hsy78957_0f.htm.

168 Ibid.

169 David W. Cash, "Distributed Assessment Systems: An Emerging Paradigm of Research, Assessment and Decision-Making for Environmental Change," *Global Environmental Change* 10, no. 4 (2000): 241.

170 Suraje Dessai, Mike Hulme, Robert Lempert, and Roger Pielke Jr "Climate Prediction: A Limit to Adaptation," in *Adapting to Climate Change: Thresholds, Values, Governance*, ed. W. Neill Adger, Irene Lorenzoni, and Karen L. O'Brien (Cambridge: Cambridge University Press, 2009), 72.

171 Herbert A. Simon, *Reason in Human Affairs* (Oxford: Basil Blackwell, 1983), 22.

172 E. Wollenberg, David Edmunds, and Louise Buck, "Using Scenarios to Make Decisions about the Future: Anticipatory Learning for the Adaptive Co-Management of Community Forests," *Landscape and Urban Planning* 47, no. 1–2 (2000): 65–77, https://doi.org/10.1016/S0169-2046(99)00071-7; Garry D. Peterson, T. Douglas Beard Jr., Beatrix E. Beisner, Elena M. Bennett, Stephen R. Carpenter, Graeme S. Cumming, C. Lisa Dent, and Tanya D. Havlicek, "Assessing Future Ecosystem Services: A Case Study of the Northern Highlands Lake District, Wisconsin," *Conservation Ecology* 7, no. 3 (2003): 1; Elena Bennett, Steve Carpenter, Steve Cork, Garry Peterson, Gerhardt Petschel-Held, Teresa Ribeiro, Monika Zurek, "Scenarios for Ecosystem Services: Rationale and Overview," in *Ecosystems and Human Well-Being: Volume 2, Scenarios. Findings of the Scenarios Working Group* (Washington, DC: Island Press, 2005); Erin L. Bohensky, Belinda Reyers, and Albert S. Van Jaarsveld, "Future Ecosystem Services in a Southern African River Basin: A Scenario Planning Approach to Uncertainty," *Conservation Biology* 20, no. 4 (2006): 1051–1061, https://doi.org/10.1111/j.1523-1739.2006.00475.x; Coreau, et al., "The Rise of Research on Futures in Ecology: Rebalancing Scenarios and Predictions."

173 Resilience Alliance, *Assessing and Managing Resilience in Social-Ecological Systems: A Practitioners Workbook. Version 1.0 June 2007* (Stockholm: Resilience Alliance, 2007).

174 Peterson et al., "Assessing Future Ecosystem Services: A Case Study of the Northern Highlands Lake District, Wisconsin," 362.

175 Robert J. Lempert and Michael E. Schlesinger, "Robust Strategies for Abating Climate Change," *Climatic Change* 45, no. 3 (2000): 387–401.

176 Dessai et al., "Climate Prediction: A Limit to Adaptation," 75.

177 Peterson et al., "Assessing Future Ecosystem Services: A Case Study of the Northern Highlands Lake District, Wisconsin," 362.

178 Basel Committee on Banking Supervision, *Principles for the Effective Management and Supervision of Climate-Related Financial Risks* (Bank of International Settlements, June 2022), 7.

179 The TCFD also makes this distinction. It defines "scenario analysis" as "a process for identifying and assessing potential implications of a range of plausible future states under conditions of uncertainty." It defines "sensitivity analysis" as "statistical analysis that examines the change in a desired output relative to a change in input parameters." Task Force on Climate-related Financial Disclosures, "Guidance on risk management integration and disclosure," 2020, 44.

180 Ascher, Steelman, and Healy, *Knowledge and Environmental Policy: Re-Imagining the Boundaries of Science and Politics*, 190.

181 Pielke, Sarewitz, and Byerly Jr., "Decision Making and the Future of Nature: Understanding and Using Predictions"; Ronald Brunner, Toddi A. Steelman, Lindy Coe-Juell, Christina M. Cromley, Christine M. Edwards, and Donna W. Tucker, *Adaptive Governance: Integrating Science, Policy, and Decision Making* (New York: Columbia University Press, 2005); Brunner and Lynch, *Adaptive Governance and Climate Change*.

182 Gunderson and Holling, *Panarchy: Understanding Transformations in Human and Natural Systems*; Fikret Berkes, Johan Colding, and Carl Folke, eds., *Navigating Social-Ecological Systems: Building Resilience for Complexity and Change* (Cambridge: Cambridge University Press, 2003); Folke, "Resilience: The Emergence of a Perspective for Social-Ecological Systems Analyses"; F. Stuart Chapin III, Gary P. Kofinas, Carl Folke, Stephen R. Carpenter, Per Olsson, Nick Abel, Reinette Biggs, Rosamond L. Naylor, Evelyn Pinkerton, D. Mark Stafford (Smith), Will Steffen, Brian Walker, and Oran R. Young, "Resilience-Based Stewardship: Strategies for Navigating Sustainable Pathways in

a Changing World," in *Principles of Ecosystem Stewardship: Resilience-Based Natural Resource Management in a Changing World*, ed. F. Stuart Chapin III, Gary P. Kofinas, and C. Folke (New York: Springer, 2009), 319–338.

183   Will L. Steffen, Angelina Sanderson, Peter Tyson, Jill Jäger, Pamela Matson, Berrien Moore, Frank Oldfield, Katherine Richardson, H. John Schellnhuber, B. L. Turner, and Robert J. Wasson, *Global Change and the Earth System: A Planet under Pressure* (New York: Springer, 2004), 286.

184   Ibid.

185   Ascher, Steelman, and Healy, *Knowledge and Environmental Policy: Re-Imagining the Boundaries of Science and Politics*, 53.

186   Gunderson, "Ecological Resilience–in Theory and Application," 433.

187   Kai Lee, *Compass and Gyroscope: Integrating Science and Politics for the Environment* (Washington: Island Press, 1993), 6, emphasis in original.

188   Jonathan Kusel, Sam C. Doak, Susan Carpenter, and Victoria E. Sturtevant, "The Role of the Public in Adaptive Ecosystem Management," in *Sierra Nevada Ecosystem Project: Final Report to Congress, Vol. II, Assessments and Scientific Basis for Management Options* (Davis: University of California Centers for Water and Wildland Resources, 1996), 611–622; Clyde F. Kiker, J. Walter Milon, and Alan W. Hodges, "Adaptive Learning for Science-Based Policy: The Everglades Restoration," *Ecological Economics* 37 (2001): 403–416; H. C. Biggs and Keven H. Rogers, "An Adaptive System to Link Science, Monitoring, and Management in Practice," in *The Kruger Experience: Ecology and Management of Savanna Heterogeneity*, ed. Johan T. du Toit, Kevin H. Rogers, and Harry C. Biggs (Washington: Island Press, 2003); George Stankey, Bernard T. Bormann, and Roger N. Clark, *Learning to Manage a Complex Ecosystem: Adaptive Management and the Northwest Forest Plan* (Portland: United Stated Department of Agriculture: Forest Service Pacific Northwest Research Station, 2006),

http://www.fs.fed.us/pnw/pubs/pnw_rp567.pdf; C. Pahl-Wostl, "The Implications of Complexity for Integrated Resources Management," *Environmental Modelling & Software* 22, no. 5 (2007): 561–569, https://doi.org/10.1016/j.envsoft.2005.12.024; Derek R. Armitage, Melissa Marschke, and Ryan Plummer, "Adaptive Co-Management and the Paradox of Learning," *Global Environmental Change* 18, no. 1 (2008): 86–98, https://doi.org/10.1016/j.gloenvcha.2007.07.002; Craig R. Allen, Joseph J. Fontaine, Kevin L. Pope, and Ahjond S. Garmestani, "Adaptive Management for a Turbulent Future," *Journal of Environmental Management* 92, no. 5 (2011): 1339–1345, https://doi.org/10.1016/j.jenvman.2010.11.019.

189 Catherine Allan and George Stankey H., *Adaptive Environmental Management: A Practitioner's Guide* (Dordrecht: Springer Science + Business Media, 2009), 5.

190 Jon Norberg and Graeme S. Cumming, "Introduction to Part 4: Practical Approaches," in *Complexity Theory for a Sustainable Future*, ed. J. Norberg and Graeme Cumming (New York: Columbia University Press, 2008), 207–208.

191 J. Edward Russo and Paul J. H. Schoemaker, "Managing Overconfidence," *Sloan Management Review* 33, no. 2 (1992): 10.

192 Derek R. Armitage, Melissa Marschke, and Ryan Plummer, "Adaptive Co-Management and the Paradox of Learning," *Global Environmental Change* 18, no. 1 (2008): 86–98, https://doi.org/10.1016/j.gloenvcha.2007.07.002; Claudia Pahl-Wostl, "A Conceptual Framework for Analysing Adaptive Capacity and Multi-Level Learning Processes in Resource Governance Regimes," *Global Environmental Change* 19, no. 3 (2009): 354–365, https://doi.org/10.1016/j.gloenvcha.2009.06.001.

193 Meg Keen, Valerie A. Brown, and Rob Dyball, "Social Learning: A New Approach to Environmental Management," in *Social Learning in Environmental Management: Towards a Sustainable Future*, ed. Meg

Keen, Valerie A. Brown, and Rob Dyball (New York: Earthscan, 2005), 3–21; Armitage, Marschke, and Plummer, "Adaptive Co-Management and the Paradox of Learning"; Claudia Pahl-Wostl, "A Conceptual Framework for Analysing Adaptive Capacity and Multi-Level Learning Processes in Resource Governance Regimes," *Global Environmental Change* 19, no. 3 (2009): 354–365, https://doi.org/10.1016/j.gloenvcha.2009.06.001.

194 Pahl-Wostl, "A Conceptual Framework for Analysing Adaptive Capacity and Multi-Level Learning Processes in Resource Governance Regimes," 359.

195 Stankey, Bormann, and Clark, "Learning to Manage a Complex Ecosystem: Adaptive Management and the Northwest Forest Plan"; Lawton, "Ecology, Politics, and Policy"; Dave Owen, "Legal Constraints, Environmental Variability, and the Limits of Innovative Environmental Governance," *Environmental Science & Policy* 12 (2009): 684–93; Lance Gunderson and Stephen S. Light, "Adaptive Management and Adaptive Governance in the Everglades Ecosystem," *Policy Sciences* 39, no. 4 (2006): 323–334, https://doi.org/10.1007/s11077-006-9027-2.

196 Charles E. Lindblom, "The Science of 'Muddling Through,'" *Public Administration Review* 19, no. 2 (1959): 79–88; Ray Hilborn, "Institutional Learning and Spawning Channels for Sockeye Salmon (Oncorhynchus Nerka)," *Canadian Journal of Fisheries and Aquatic Sciences* 49, no. 6 (1992): 1126–1136; Lance Gunderson, "Resilience, Flexibility and Adaptive Management - - Antidotes for Spurious Certitude?," *Conservation Ecology* 3 (1999): 7; Stephen Dovers, "Processes and Institutions for Environmental Management: Why and How to Analyse," in *Managing Australia's Environment*, ed. Stephen Dovers and Su Wild River (Sydney: The Federation Press, 2003), 3–12.

197 Brenda Taylor, Laurie Kremsater, and Rick Ellis, *Adaptive Management of Forests in British Columbia* (Victoria: British Columbia Ministry of Forests - Forest Practices Branch, 1997), 5, http://www.for.gov.bc.ca/hfd/pubs/docs/sil/sil426.pdf.

198 J. B. Ruhl, "Regulation by Adaptive Management-Is It Possible?," *Minnesota Journal of Law, Science & Technology* 7, no. 1 (2005): 21–57.

199 Boksalis, "Sustainability report 2021," 2021, 61, https://boskalis.com/media/13vdu5zw/boskalis_sustainability_report_2021_lr-2.pdf.

200 Donald T. Campbell, "Reforms as Experiments," in *Readings in Evaluation Research*, ed. Francis G. Caro (New York: Russell Sage Foundation, 1971), 234.

201 Gordon L. Baskerville, "The Forestry Problem: Adaptive Lurches of Renewal," in *Barriers & Bridges to the Renewal of Ecosystems and Institutions,* ed. Lance H. Gunderson, C. S. Holling, and Stephen S. Light, (New York: Columbia University Press, 1995); Cindy L. Halbert, "How Adaptive Is Adaptive Management? Implementing Adaptive Management in Washington State and British Columbia," *Reviews in Fisheries Science* 1, no. 3 (1993): 261–283, https://doi.org/10.1080/10641269309388545; Taylor, Kremsater, and Ellis, "Adaptive Management of Forests in British Columbia"; Sandy Paton, Allan Curtis, Geoff McDonald, and Mary Woods, "Regional Natural Resource Management: Is It Sustainable?," *Australasian Journal of Environmental Management* 11, no. 4 (2004): 259–267; Stefan Hajkowicz, "The Evolution of Australia's Natural Resource Management Programs: Towards Improved Targeting and Evaluation of Investments," *Land Use Policy* 26, no. 2 (2009): 471–478, https://doi.org/10.1016/j.landusepol.2008.06.004.

202 Holling, "What Barriers? What Bridges?," 8.

203 Stephen Dovers, *Environment and Sustainability Policy: Creation, Implementation, Evaluation* (Annandale: Federation Press, 2005).

204 Gunderson, "Resilience, Flexibility and Adaptive Management – Antidotes for Spurious Certitude?," 5.

205 Ibid.

206 Brunner and Lynch, *Adaptive Governance and Climate Change*, 41.

207 Global Reporting Initiative, "Our mission and history," 2024, https://www.globalreporting.org/about-gri/mission-history/.

208 Global Reporting Initiative, "Sustainability reporting guidelines: Version 3.1," 2011, 8.

209 IFRS Foundation, "SASB Standards: About Us," 2024, https://sasb.ifrs.org/about/.

210 This was unlikely to be SASB's intent. SASB's Conceptual Framework acknowledged the interdependency between sustainability and corporate value creation at a more fundamental level than a collection of disparate risks.

211 Carol A. Adams et al., "The Double-Materiality Concept: Application and Issues" (Global Reporting Initiative, 2021), 8, https://www.globalreporting.org/media/jrbntbyv/griwhitepaper-publications.pdf.

212 As quoted in Jennifer Radden, *The Nature of Melancholy* (Oxford University Press, 2002), https://doi.org/10.1093/acprof:oso/9780195151657.001.0001.

213 Elaine Cohen, "23 Sustainability Reporting Insights for 2023," *Csr-Reporting: Thoughts and Insights about Social and Environmental Responsibility and Sustainability Reporting* (blog), December 28, 2022, https://csr-reporting.blogspot.com/2022/12/23-sustainability-reporting-insights.html?m=1.

214 Impact Management Platform, "The Imperative for Impact Management: Clarifying the Relationship between Impacts, System-Wide Risk and Materiality," June 2023, v.

215 Impact Management Platform, v.

216 International Integrated Reporting Council, "Towards Integrated Reporting: Communicating Value in the 21st Century," 2011, 7.

217 International Integrated Reporting Council, "Towards Integrated Reporting: Communicating Value in the 21st Century," 2011, 5.

218 "Fortune 500: 1975 Full List," 2021.

219 International Integrated Reporting Council, "International <IR> Framework," January 2021; Committee of Sponsoring Organizations of the Treadway Commission and World Business Council for Sustainable Development, "Enterprise risk management: applying enterprise risk management to environmental, social and governance-related risks," October 2018.

220 Global Reporting Initiative, "Sustainability Reporting Guidelines: Version 3.1," 8.

221 EFRAG, "Implementation guidance for the materiality assessment," August 23, 2023, 31.

222 International Sustainability Standards Board, "IFRS S1 general requirements for disclosure of sustainability-related financial information," June 2022, 6.

223 Committee of Sponsoring Organizations of the Treadway Commission and World Business Council for Sustainable Development, "Enterprise risk management: applying enterprise risk management to environmental, social and governance-related risks," 28.

224 Eliot Metzger Samantha Putt Del Pino, Sally Prowitt, Jenna Goodward, and Alexander Perera, *sSWOT: A Sustainability SWOT* (World Resources Institute, December 2012).

225 For additional information on biases affecting corporate sustainability analyses, see Committee of Sponsoring Organizations of the Treadway Commission and World Business Council for Sustainable Develop-

ment, "Enterprise risk management: applying enterprise risk management to environmental, social and governance-related risks," 65.

226 For additional guidance and examples of how to map the value chain and identify dependencies and impacts, see dralexgold.com or Chapter 2 of Committee of Sponsoring Organizations of the Treadway Commission and World Business Council for Sustainable Development, "Enterprise risk management: applying enterprise risk management to environmental, social and governance-related risks."

227 For example, IFRS S1 paragraph 55 suggests that companies may consider sustainability-related risks and opportunities identified by peers in the same industries and regions.

228 ESG Navigator can be accessed at esgnavigator.com.

229 COSO/WBCSD guidance mentioned several times in this chapter cautions against overreliance on numeric evidence, given the risk of overlooking sustainability impacts and dependencies that are not easily quantified.

230 International Integrated Reporting Council, "International <IR> Framework"; Coalition for Inclusive Capitalism, "EPIC: the embankment project for inclusive capitalism," 2018.

231 Relevant guidance often distinguishes between outcomes and impacts. Although an important distinction, I will not expand on it further in this book. My main interest is highlighting the difference between conventional reporting (focused on inputs and outputs only), and any kind of outcome reporting.

232 Taskforce on Nature-related Financial Disclosures, "Guidance on scenario analysis: version 1.0," September 2023, https://tnfd.global/wp-content/uploads/2023/09/Guidance_on_scenario_analysis_V1.pdf?v=1695138235.

233 For example, International Sustainability Standards Board, "IFRS S1 General Requirements for Disclosure of Sustainability-related Financial Information."

234 IFRS S2 Climate-related Disclosures paragraph B11 states that publicly available climate-related scenarios—from authoritative sources—that describe future trends and a range of pathways to plausible outcomes are considered to be available to the entity without undue cost or effort.

235 IPCC, *Global Warming of 1.5°C: IPCC Special Report on Impacts of Global Warming of 1.5°C above Pre-Industrial Levels in Context of Strengthening Response to Climate Change, Sustainable Development, and Efforts to Eradicate Poverty*, 1st ed. (Cambridge University Press, 2022), https://doi.org/10.1017/9781009157940.

236 Examples of scenarios across various temperature outcomes are available at dralexgold.com.

237 Some recent standards ask for companies to include a scenario that limits warming to under 1.5°C (e.g., European Sustainability Reporting Standards).

238 I am indebted to XRB of New Zealand for contributing the scenario archetype language into the field, which has helped clarify the differences between the various scenarios at various points in the process. https://www.xrb.govt.nz/dmsdocument/4994

239 For example, an asset manager from Abrdn was quoted in Environmental Finance: "many of the widely used models for projecting future impacts of the energy transition—including NGFS scenarios—are of limited use for investors as they fail to project the most likely level of warming" Michael Hurley, "What Next for Climate Scenarios?," *Environmental Finance*, October 12, 2023, sec. Analysis, https://www. environmental-finance.com/content/analysis/what-next-for-climate-scenarios.html.

240 In addition to the TCFD, other guidance discouraging the identification of a most likely scenario includes the New Zealand External Review Board and the Bank of International Settlements, in addition to the academic literature cited in chapter 5.

241 Task Force on Climate-related Financial Disclosures, "Implementing the recommendations of the Task Force on Climate-Related Financial Disclosures," 2021.

242 Ibid., 59.

243 Byerly, "Prepared Statement of Radford Byerly, Jr."

244 TSMC, "TCFD report," 2022, https://esg.tsmc.com/en-US/sustainable-management/tcfd-disclosure.

245 Ibid.

246 Task Force on Climate-related Financial Disclosures, "Guidance on risk management integration and disclosure," 11.

247 Ecofys, The Generation Foundation, and CDP, *How-to Guide to Corporate Internal Carbon Pricing - Four Dimensions to Best Practice Approaches* (Carbon Pricing Unlocked Partnership, December 2017), https://cdn.cdp.net/cdp-production/cms/reports/documents/000/002/740/original/cpu-2017-how-to-guide-to-internal-carbon-pricing.pdf?1521554897.

248 Rasmus Heltberg, Paul Bennett Siegel, and Steen Lau Jorgensen, "Addressing Human Vulnerability to Climate Change: Toward a No-Regrets Approach," Global Environmental Change 19, no. 1 (2009): 89–99, https://doi.org/10.1016/j.gloenvcha.2008.11.003.

249 Brunner and Lynch, *Adaptive Governance and Climate Change*, 207.

250 University of Colorado at Boulder, "Two degrees of warming already baked in," Science Daily, July 31, 2017, https://www.sciencedaily.com/releases/2017/07/170731114534.htm.

251 This distinction between resilience assessment and scenario analysis is a developing area at the time of publishing this book (the year 2024). Additional information on resilience assessment and scenario analysis is available at dralexgold.com.

252 Chief Executives for Corporate Purpose, "11th Annual Board of Boards Executive report: competing for the long run," New York, February 29, 2016.

253 Emmanuel Faber, "Resilience is the new efficiency," LinkedIn, April 15, 2023, https://www.linkedin.com/posts/emmanuelfaber_hec-talks-la-résilience-comme-nouvel-impératif-activity-6988111024767803392-I5Nw. Faber states, "Resilience is the new efficiency. Climate change will redefine economics and competitive advantage. Getting prepared: in Montreal this week for our International Sustainability Standards Board (ISSB) redeliberations on foundational and climate standards for global capital markets."

254 The "first set of ISSB Standards" refers to IFRS S1 general requirements for sustainability-related financial disclosures and IFRS S2 climate-related disclosures.

255 Emmanuel Faber, "ISSB Chair Emmanuel Faber at the IFRS Foundation Conference: a new common language to build more resilient economics," IFRS Foundation Conference, June 26, 2023.

256 Francis Fukuyama, *The Origins of Political Order: From Prehuman Times to the French Revolution* (New York: Farrar, Straus and Giroux, 2012), 36.

257 McGilchrist, *The Master and His Emissary: The Divided Brain and the Making of the Western World*, 229.

258 Peter Cripps, "ISSB stakeholders want more information about materiality," Environmental Finance, September 13, 2022, sec. Analysis, https://www.environmental-finance.com/content/analysis/issb-stakeholders-want-more-information-about-materiality.html.

259 Recommendation *Strategy (c)* asks businesses to "describe the resilience of the organization's strategy, taking into consideration different climate-related scenarios." Task Force on Climate-related Financial Disclosures, "Recommendations of the Task Force on Climate-Related Financial Disclosures: final report," June 2017.

260 IFRS S1 paragraph 41, and IFRS S2 paragraph 22. International Sustainability Standards Board, "IFRS S1 general requirements for disclosure of sustainability-related financial information," June 2022; International Sustainability Standards Board, "IFRS S2 climate-related disclosures," June 2022.

261 For example, ESRS 2, General Disclosures, paragraph 48(f). European Commission, "Commission Delegated Regulation (EU) Supplementing Directive 2013/34/EU of the European Parliament and of the Council as Regards Sustainability Reporting Standards: Annex I European Sustainability Reporting Standards (ESRS)," Brussels, July 31, 2023.

262 I am grateful to personal communication with Janine Guilliot, former CEO of SASB, and the Value Reporting Foundation, and her insight that the category of "metrics and targets" is better referred to as the process of performance measurement.

263 CDP, GRI, Sustainability Accounting Standards Board, International Integrated Reporting Council Industry Group, "Reporting on enterprise value: illustrated with a prototype climate-related financial disclosure standard," December 2020, 7.

264 American Chemical Society International Historic Chemical Landmarks, "Joseph Priestley and the discovery of oxygen," 2024, https://www.acs.

org/education/whatischemistry/landmarks/josephpriestleyoxygen. html.

265 American Chemical Society International Historic Chemical Landmarks.

266 Ibid.

267 American Chemical Society International Historic Chemical Landmarks, "The chemical revolution of Antoine-Laurent Lavoisier," 2024, https://www.acs.org/education/whatischemistry/landmarks/ lavoisier.html.

268 This quote is commonly attributed to Einstein, for example, see Albert Einstein, "Everything should be made as simple as possible, but not simpler," ForbesQuotes (blog), 2024, https://www.forbes.com/ quotes/193/. For a review of the debate on whether the words actually came from Einstein himself, see Garson O'Toole, "Everything should be made as simple as possible, but not simpler," Quote Investigator (blog), May 13, 2011, https://quoteinvestigator.com/2011/05/13/ einstein-simple/.